A LIFE OF MANY COLORS

From Israel to America

Miki Z. Bell

A LIFE OF MANY COLORS

Dedication

This book represents my deep gratitude to GOD for protecting me and being there for me.

To my children Robert Scott Bell and my daughter Julia Bell Guise, and to my four grandchildren Jeremy and Benjamin Guise and Elijah and Ariana Bell.

To my sisters Ruth Grant and Nava Shacham and my nieces, nephews and cousins.

I thank you for having played such an important part in my life and for being you.

I share my experiences with you through this book, in the hope that your life will thereby be enriched.

May you always live with gratitude and love in your hearts.

Acknowledgements

To my friends who were always there when I needed them, and you know who you are.

To my business friends who supported me and believed in me while I was building my business as an entrepreneur.

To my neighbor and friend Shawn Flynn whom I consider my angel, for always helping me with computer problems as I was writing my book, and always taking care of my cats when I travel.

To Ann McIndoo, my Coach for encouraging me to get this book out of my head and into a book form.

To my friend Linda Kedy for her proofreads input and corrections.

To my dancing friends at the West Coast Swing Club for bringing me so much joy through dancing.

To ESS, Executive Suite Singles Club, for being there as an extended family to me.

To author Aubrey Rose, for his input and suggestions for this book, and whose advice I cherish.

Contents

Chapter One
In the Beginning - Childhood... 1

Chapter Two
Meeting My Husband... 51

Photos.. 61

Chapter Three
Life in Georgia 1975.. 65

Chapter Four
Introduction to Convention Work.................................. 71

Chapter Five
I Find a Buyer for Miki Bell Enterprises, Inc................ 85

Chapter Six
Creating ISBPS.. 89

Chapter Seven
Flashback – Visits to Israel... 95

Chapter Eight
My Sister's Devastating Accident................................ 102

Chapter Nine
Back to Meeting Luc Chaltin the Homeopath............ 106

Chapter Ten
Looking to Meet Someone.. 122

Chapter Eleven
Dating and Dancing.. 125

Chapter Twelve
The Secret to Good Health and My Life's Philosophy 131

Foreword

This is a well told story of one life, multi-faceted and multi-colored. What emerges is sheer enthusiasm, a love of life, a willingness to follow new paths, but always with positive attitude.

The author has been a seamstress, hairdresser, police official, air hostess, realtor, Convention organizer, director of an homeopathic enterprise, bringing to every sphere that bubbling enthusiasm, self discipline, enjoyment of both work and people.

The story ranges from Tel-Aviv to Atlanta, noting public events en route, but above all, the undulation of personal relationships with parents, sisters, husbands, children, et al, and ending brightly with her love of dancing combined with her views as to how to live ones life.

It is a stimulating tale and the author can take credit for her achievement.

Aubrey Rose C.B.E. D. University

Note: Aubrey Rose is the author of many books some of which are: "The Rainbow Never Ends", "Brief Encounters of a Legal Kind", "Journey Into Imortality", and a recent childrens book entitled "Sea Olympics, as above so below".

The title of CBE has been bestowed on him by the the Queen of England. I am so grateful to him for writing the forward to my book.

Chapter One

In the Beginning - Childhood

I was born Miriam Turgeman (Miki) on January 29, 1934, in Tel Aviv, Israel.

I have a sister, Ruth, who is 5½ years older than me, and another sister, Nava, born to my father from his second wife, Adel. A brother, Eli, was also born to my father and Adel. Unfortunately, Eli passed on at age 13 after an illness called Cushing Syndrome that affects the pituitary glands.

My father, Moshe Turgeman, a Sephardic Jew, was an eighth generation Israeli. His father, my grandfather Rabbi Yitzhak Turgeman, was born in Chevron in 1875 and died in 1956.

My father was born to a long and entrenched family of rabbis in the Holy Land. My great grandfather, Rabbi Israel Turgeman, married the granddaughter of the esteemed and famous Rabbi Levi Yitzhak of Berdichev.

Thanks to the excellent education my grandfather received in the Ottoman Turkish schools than in charge of the land, he spoke Turkish, Arabic, and Hebrew. He was the first Jewish employee in the Chevron municipality during the Turkish occupation. He was later transferred to the city of Yaffo and worked there in a high official capacity as judge under the British Mandatory Government, which gave him the ability to help many Jews who suffered under the Turks and the British. He also built a synagogue, Netzah Israel, to commemorate his father. It still stands on Ben-Yehuda Street in Tel Aviv.

My father had four brothers and two sisters. The oldest brother, Raphael, was the apple of my grandmother's eye, but he was greedy, a crook, and a child molester.

My mother, Rachel Zak (Sack), came to Palestine when she was 16. She was an Ashkenazi Jew born in Lithuania and spoke 8 languages fluently. She had a very harsh childhood in Europe during the period of the pogrom and World War I. She was a survivor. My mother had two sisters and one brother, their names were Luba, Avrom, and Bella.

My parents' background and culture were world apart. Sephardic Jews are originally of Spanish and Portuguese culture, while Ashkenazi Jews are of an Eastern European culture. These two cultures did not mix very well, and hence, at a time when divorce was almost unheard of, my parents separated and divorced.

Where I Grew Up - My Neighborhood

My parents owned an apartment building they had built at 23 Frug Street in Tel-Aviv. It was a three-story building with six apartments. Each apartment had three bedrooms, a kitchen, a bathroom, a separate toilet, and a balcony. One entered the apartment through the front door into a long corridor that connected each of the rooms in the apartment.

My mother did not like having debts or a mortgage, so she convinced my father to sell half the building and pay off the mortgage, which he did.

Our street and the adjacent streets of Gordon & Dov Hoz were known as the Habimah Compound. Habimah was and still is the Israeli National Theater, established in Moscow in 1918 and then in Israel in 1936.

Music, theater, dance, and art galleries, which I absorbed by osmosis, surrounded me. My mother did not have much interest in the arts, but I certainly did.

Memories Prior to the Kidnapping

I remember having a life-size doll with a beautiful baby carriage. My doll could open and close her eyes, and she could also cry if you pressed her belly. The doll was imported from Germany. I loved playing with that doll. I would collect sheets, pillows, and blankets to create a tent in our balcony and this would be my refuge into the world of make-believe. My doll's name was Shoshi.

I also remember playing with the kids my age on our street. I loved to play, and also liked to eat. Our apartment was on the third floor, and every couple of hours I would call to my mother from the yard asking her to throw down a sandwich of bread, butter, and jelly. She would wrap it and throw it down from the window, and then I would catch it and continue playing while eating my sandwich. The games we would play were hide-and-seek, jumping rope, and cops-and-robbers. We would also collect and play with marbles.

I loved eating bananas. When my mother came home from the market with a few kilos of bananas, I would grab about four bananas, lock myself in the bathroom, eat all the bananas, and then come out with the banana skins. I can't remember getting into trouble for doing this.

We had a grocery store on our street, a few houses from ours. I would go in the morning to get the freshly-baked rye bread, which was still warm, and I would start nibbling on the bread on the way home. It was the most delicious bread I ever remember eating. The crust was crunchy and delicious.

Each customer at this grocery store had a page in which the owner would write down the purchase and the amount due. Once a week my mother would settle the bill with the owner. It was so nice that you were always greeted by your name, and everyone knew each other. I had lots of girlfriends on our street and we would often play in the street or at someone's home.

Sometimes, we would play tricks on the people strolling down the street. One of the tricks we did was filling a can with water, tying it to a string, putting the can on a fence, and tying the string to a power pole. When people passed by, they wouldn't notice the string, and the can would drop by their feet and get their feet wet. We would hide behind the bushes, and we had a good laugh every time this happened.

We had an open field across the street before a house was built on it in later years. We collected sticks and made a bonfire. We would bring potatoes from home and bake them in the bonfire. The potatoes would be delicious to eat, all burned on the outside and the inside soft and delicious. Our street was very safe and friendly to kids.

Every apartment had an icebox to keep the food from spoiling in the summer heat. This was before refrigerators were invented. A horse-and-buggy vendor of ice blocks would come down the street several times a week, and we would buy a quarter-block of ice to put in the icebox. There was a tray at the bottom of the ice-box that collected the melted water from the ice and was emptied every other day. The ice was cut with a pick, and as it was being cut, fragments of ice dropped to the ground. We would pick up the ice pieces and suck them; it was so refreshing during the hot summers.

The Kidnapping

When I was about 5½ my father kidnapped my older sister, Ruth and me. I remember my father telling us that we were going out for a picnic to Ramat Gan. It was a sunny Saturday, and Ramat Gan is known for its beautiful gardens just outside Tel-Aviv.

I was excited about this outing with my father and sister. It was rare that we had fun with our parents. I asked excitedly if we should prepare food to take along, but my father said that this was taken care of by my Aunt Rachel, and she would meet us there.

I wore a light flowery summer dress and so did my sister. We wore sandals since it was a warm summer day, and off we went, going up Gordon Street to Ben Yehuda Street to take the #4 bus. This was just a couple of blocks from our house. We climbed on the bus, going north. The fourth stop was Jabotinsky Street.

My father said we must get off there; I did not understand why. "Father, this is not Ramat-Gan yet," I said. Father replied that we are going to visit my grandmother first and would understand why later. So we got off the bus and walked to #3 Jabotinsky Street and up to grandmother's apartment on the third floor.

The house was one block from the Mediterranean Sea. From the balcony I could see the beautiful view of the sea. I loved the sea and the sea breeze. My grandfather, who owned quite a bit of real estate in Tel-Aviv, owned the house. I remember hearing as a child that my grandfather donated to the city of Tel-Aviv the land that is used as the cemetery for dignitaries on Trumpeldor Street in Tel-Aviv. I think he is also buried there.

I went straight to the balcony and stared at the sea. I don't remember what explanation was given for not going to the promised picnic, but I do remember that for the next 3½ years we lived at our grandmother's house.

Life at Grandmother's

After the first few months, grandmother, grandfather, and their favorite and oldest son, Raphael, moved to another house further south in Tel-Aviv to number 75 Nachalat Benyamin Street. Grandfather also owned this house.

It was fall with winter approaching when we moved, and we only had summer clothes. We needed our winter coats and shoes, and my father was trying to get these from our mother. However, she said we could get our winter coats and shoes only if we come back home. She was holding our warm coats as ransom.

While at my grandmother's, I was told horrible stories about my mother, and I was left with a feeling that my mother was a bad person. I remember a shivering feeling going through my spine when her name was mentioned.

A court battle ensued between my parents, as to who would get custody of us. I was kept at home, while my sister continued going to school. She was older and therefore was allowed to continue her classes. My father was afraid that if I went to school, my mother would find out where I was and would take me back.

I was kept away from school for close to a year and was used as a maid for my grandmother. I would go to the grocery store to bring items she needed for her cooking, I would wash the floors, help do the laundry by hand, (there were no washing machines or clothes dryers then), hang the laundry on the line in the sun to dry.

I had to stand on a bucket in order to reach the line and attach the clothespin to the clothes. I also had to clean the rugs. My grandmother had very large Persian rugs. My sister and I would take the rugs once a week to the large balcony; we cleaned and brushed the rugs with water and vinegar to make them shine.

When my sister returned from school I felt more secure with her around. She was the only constant person in my life and the only one I could trust at the time.

My father would go to work, and I was left to the whims of my grandmother and her oldest son, Raphael, whom she adored and worshiped over all her other children. Raphael had a room with a private entrance; in fact he had whatever he wanted.

I remember that he would call me to come visit him in the morning, he asked me to come to the bed and lie beside him for a cuddle. He would press himself against me from behind, and I would feel something hard pushing against me, and then it would feel damp and disgusting. I would get up and run away to clean myself. This abuse continued for some time, but I cannot remember for how long. I must have blocked much of the experience out of my mind. I felt ashamed and confused about what was being done to me by my uncle. I did not tell anyone about this abuse; I was too scared to tell about it to my sister or to my father. All I knew was that I had to obey Raphael's wishes, or I would suffer the consequences from my grandmother.

Raphael was short, had curly hair, and was about 5′ 4″. He wore thick rimmed glasses, had crooked teeth, and was ugly in more ways than one. He later got married and had two children, a son and a daughter Yitzhak called Itzik and Rachel who are my first cousins. I doubt that they know what their father was really like before they were born. They are the benefactors of much of the property their father stole from his siblings.

Grandmother was a short stocky women about 4′ 8″ with no shape to her body; she always wore a loose fitting house dress with an apron over it. Her face was wrinkled, she had a pointed nose with a pointed chin, small lips in between, and it looked as if her nose could touch her pointed chin. She had small eyes, false teeth which were more often in a glass of water rather than in her mouth. She suffered from headaches, and I remember her always having a wet cloth tied around her forehead. She would say "ya rassi," which means "my head" in Arabic. She was uneducated, and when she needed to sign her name, she would sign with her thumb print. In those days, Sephardic women were not educated; they were used to bear children, cook, and take care of the children and the husband. She spoke Arabic with her children, and her Hebrew was not very good.

She was, however, a magnificent cook. You could lick your fingers after eating her food, altough she was very stingy with her portions. She wanted to make sure that Raphael had all he wanted and more. Ruthie and I, on the other hand, would always leave the table hungry.

I remember standing in the kitchen and watching when she would serve the portions of food onto the plates. She would put food in my plate and my sister's plate, would stare at it and then remove some of the food with her fingers and back into the pot. I wanted to scream, "Please don't remove any, I want it all," but it would do me no good. I was just a little maid to her and she was devoid of any affection for either of us. She was only concerned that her Raphael would have as much as he wanted.

My father was a kind and good man, but he had no idea how we were treated. He lived in a room in the attic of this house. He would go to work, come home after work, eat, and go to his room in the attic and to bed. He always seemed worried, so we didn't want to add to his worries by complaining how we were treated by his mother.

Description of Our Environment at Grandmother's

The apartment we lived in was very spacious. Grandfather owned the entire building. On the ground floor was a private orthodox school called Beit Jacob Hachadash, meaning The New Jacob House. On the second floor were the living quarters of grandmother and grandfather including a very spacious living room, which Raphael used as his office.

The living room had a couch against the wall on which my sister and I slept at night together. A short corridor led to grandmother and grandfathers' bedroom, to the kitchen, bathroom, and to the large patio/terrace. On the opposite side was a long corridor with private entrance leading to Raphael's private quarters.

Adjacent to the apartment, on the same floor was a very large room, like a ballroom, used on Friday nights, Saturday mornings, and the High Holidays as a synagogue. My grandfather was a rabbi and also a son and grandson of rabbis. The synagogue room had separate sections for men and women, in the Orthodox Jewish tradition. The separation is so that the men will not be distracted by the women during prayer. The room had benches for sitting, and also had a stage where the Torah was housed. I remember when the Torah would be brought out of the Ark covered in blue velvet fabric with gold embroidery of the Ten Commandments on it. I liked participating in the services as it was a time I could be close to my father. The services were well attended by people, many of whom were my fathers' friends as well as family friends.

My father's room was two flights of stairs up from where we were. The climate in the summer was very hot and humid and I am sure my father was not comfortable up in the attic, but he did not complain. My sister would go up sometimes to clean his room for him.

The couch my sister and I slept on was a beige color of corduroy fabric. During the summer, which was long, hot, and humid, the couch was infested with bed bugs. We were busy weekly cleaning out the bed bugs. They would be lodged at the lines of the corduroy. We would look for them by going over each seam with our fingers.

We also had head lice. We would clean each other's hair and remove the lice one by one, like little monkeys. Sometimes it was necessary to cover our whole heads with petrol in order to kill the eggs. I even had lice in my eyelashes. I would pull them out with my fingers and crush them on the terrace cement floor with my fingernails. This was our life for 3½ years.

Our Parents in Custody Battle over Property

During these years my mother and father were in a court battle over who would get custody of us. I remember so well, one very cold and windy winter day, we were standing on a street corner at the bottom of the building where the attorney's office was. We were shivering in our summer clothes and sandals. Our mother was meeting our father at the attorney's office to decide who would get us. My mother came with our navy coats and blue winter shoes under her arm; we were shivering and hoping to get our warm coats. Half an hour went by, which seemed like an eternity. We prayed we would get our coats; we did not care who we went with, we just wanted to be warm. We saw our mother leave with our coats still under her arm. Apparently, they did not reach an agreement as to who would take us home. Thank God, we got new winter coats once our father realized mother kept our coats. I later found out that the war between them was over property. Uncle Raphael was influencing my father to keep ownership of our apartment house, while our mother wanted father to sign his part of the apartment house ownership to my sister and me. As long as he refused to do that, our mother refused to give us our warm winter coats.

Our father though very kind, was weak in nature. He was a slender man about 5′ 5″ in height, and wore black rim glasses over his kind blue eyes. He had a black Afro hairstyle and a friendly smile showing his perfect white teeth. He always dressed nicely and professionally. He was a heavy smoker, though; in those days, most people were smokers. Unfortunately, he was under the vile influence of his older brother, Raphael, who was orchestrating fathers' behavior. My father finally succumbed to my mother's requests to sign his part of the house into our names. I later found out that my sister threatened my father that if he would not sign his part to us, as our mother requested, she would commit suicide and jump off the roof. This scared our father, and he said to her, "Rutile, I'll do whatever you want." And he told Raphael, "I don't care what you think, I am signing my part of the house to Ruthie and Miki."

As I look back, I must believe that our parents were totally unaware of the pain they were inflicting on us while they were fighting the custody battle. I cannot imagine them acting that way had they been aware.

Finally Going to School

After one year of being kept at home and out of school, my father decided it might be safe to enroll me at the new Beth Jacob Orthodox school, since it was downstairs, close to home.

For six months I attended that school. The primary curriculum was prayer and studying the Torah. I would come home and recite the prayers with all the proper motions as entertainment for my sister. We were not religious at home with our mother or with grandmother, although grandfather was a rabbi. Looking back, it seems that he was more of a businessman than a rabbi. Our home did not feel religious although the Sabbath candles were lit on Friday night and we practiced the holiday traditions. But then, living in Israel, you practice and honor the religious holidays without having to be religious.

Grandfather always had a flask of arak (an alcoholic drink) in his inside pocket, and he would take a sip every now and then. His breath always smelled from alcohol. He called me Kukla. I liked him, he was kind and sweet and non-confrontational. Grandfather was a slender man about 5′ 4″ in height. He had blue eyes and had a graying mustache and gray hair.

My Relationship With God

I had and have my private and personal relationship with God. To me, God was always very much a part of me and within me. While the God that I would pray to at school or at synagogue was more distant, this is how I felt.

God resides in my heart, and He is always with me and protecting me. I feel God is my best friend. I have much love for God. I pray and thank God every night and morning and finish with," For the good of the whole, thy will be done." I know God knows better than I what is best for my family and me.

I don't much care for organized religion. However, I respect people's individual choices. The worst crimes against humanity were and are made in the name of religion. Just look at what the Muslims are doing in the name of religion. I think that if people were secure in their religious choice, they would not have to put down any religion other than theirs as some religious people do. However, the Muslim religion is another story. The Muslim ideology opposes Western culture; they consider Shariah Law superior and are committed to changing the world to a Muslim one. They have a long-range plan and are staying focused on achieving their goal. The topic of religion is quite complex, and I do not wish to cover this topic in depth, although I do have my opinions on the subject.

I belong to a Chabad synagogue and only go during the High Holidays of Rosh Hashanah and Yom Kippur. This is my way of keeping up with my Jewish identity and heritage. I also like the rabbi and his wife; they are very warm and caring people and have built a very nice and warm congregation. Their names are Rabbi Yossi and Esther Lerman.

My view of religion can be simply explained and is set out by the author Neale Donald Walsch in his books entitled, *Conversations with God*. I fully identify with his views.

I talk to God whenever and wherever I am. I do not need a structure to communicate with God. As I said, God is with me and is very much a part of me and I am forever grateful to God for whatever comes my way. I trust that the outcome will always be what I need for my own growth.

1942 - A New School

By age 7½, my father decided that I needed to go to a more traditional school and I was enrolled in the Alliance Française School, where the primary language taught was French. I was entering third grade with children who had been there since first grade studying in French, and I had no knowledge it.

My father arranged for a private tutor to help me catch up with the rest of the class. I took to French like a fish to water, and within three months I was the best student in class in French.

This made me feel very proud of myself. I enjoyed the Alliance Française School. I was finally out of the hands of grandmother, at least for a good part of the day.

We wore a uniform, which was a blue apron tied and buttoned in the back, with an emblem of the school on the left side pocket. I liked my teacher very much. Her name was Madame Machlul. She was strict, but I had no problem with that. I did my homework, and cherished the discipline. It gave me the feeling that someone cared about me.

I made some friends and we would meet to do homework at their home. It felt so good to finally have some friends and to be in a normal environment. I began to settle in and enjoy the routine of going to school, which was a welcome escape from home.

My sister had her own friends, and when she would go out, I would always be behind her . She could not go anywhere without me at her tail. When she would be at a friend's house I would always fall asleep in the corner somewhere. When it was time to go home, she or her friends would carry me.

I was a thumb sucker, and did that until the age of 12. I could not stop sucking my thumb any earlier. My left hand thumb would go in my mouth and the pointer finger on my nose the moment I would lay down. My thumb was emaciated from sucking it. My sister tried to scare me by telling me that my thumb would fall off if I did not stop sucking it. I was scared, but not enough to stop.

At night sometimes my sister would tie her hand to mine so that she could pull my hand down when it went to my mouth. She also tried to tie a bandage on it or put mustard on it, but nothing would help to make me stop.

I finally stopped sucking my thumb, when I took charge of my life and destiny. I forced myself to sleep on my hand, and that is how I was finally able to stop.

1943 - 1944 - Going Back to Mother (Age 9)

After our father signed his part ownership in the property to us, it was than decided by the court that our mother would regain custody of us, and we were to return to live with our mother. My sister told me that we were going back to live with our mother. I was scared and did not know how to handle it, I had such bad feelings about my mother and was scared of her.

I remember one day she came hoping to see me when I was at the Orthodox school. When I saw her, I ran upstairs with such fear as if I had seen a snake, and now I was told that all was okay and we were going back home.

I was scared, but my sister said it was all right, that mother knew all, and there was no need to worry. Well, as long as my sister was there, and she said it was okay, I trusted what she said. So we returned home.

My mother prepared a nice table with a clean tablecloth and made our favorite vanilla pudding to welcome us home. The tablecloth was white with hand embroidery. I have this tablecloth to this day and cherish it.

It was very difficult for me to relate or to trust my mother at this time. I was back at her home, but it did not feel like the loving home I was craving. I had seen my friends' homes and they had both parents who seemed loving and caring for their children. Mother was angry most of the time and I did not like her energy.

I was envious of the love I saw in my friends' homes, while my mother was very cold and unable to show love or affection. I had to earn her approval and acceptance of me; it was not there automatically just because I was me. I felt very distant from her. I also had no respect for her or her prejudiced views of anyone who was not like her.

I could not relate to her anger and judgment of my father. She hated Sephardic Jews, and made me ashamed of my Sephardic heritage. I was considered half Ashkenazi and half Sephardic. However, living with my mother who was Ashkenazi, I had to conform to her belief system. Mother was petite, about 4′ 8″, with light brown hair and green eyes, a slender body, and she was always well-groomed and well-dressed. She would move and walk very fast. She had a high-pitched voice and was very calculating in her relationships with people. She would be very nice, if she needed you, and not as nice if she had no use for you. I had no respect for these characteristics she possessed; it went against my grain. I was so different from her, I was honest and straightforward, probably too much so. I could not tolerate dishonesty, and to me she was phony. It was difficult living with her.

My last name was Turgeman. In Hebrew it means Interpreter, my father's name in the Sephardic community, a well-respected and revered family.

Mother, after the divorce, resumed her maiden name, which was Zak, also spelled Sack. The name Sack in Hebrew means Seed of Holiness. It was odd for me to have a different last name than my mother, since divorce was quite uncommon at the time. So, at the insistence of my mother, I legally changed my last name to Zak from Turgeman. I did that around the age 15. I am sure this must have hurt my father greatly. But for the sake of peace at home, I had to do it.

Father's Job

I loved my father. Everyone who knew him loved him. He would give you the shirt off his back if you needed it. My father worked for the British Government as a tax collector. In those days, before computers, tax collection was done by going to people's homes to collect the tax, and write a hand-written receipt with a carbon copy. Carbon copy is unknown in today's technological age. It is a paper that on one side has blue or black carbon backing, and it transfers what you have written to another paper underneath it. Hence, you have a copy of what you have written for your records.

I remember going to cafés with my father when I was about three or four. He would meet his male friends and I would go along. I liked being around my father and his friends. He also had Arab friends and would speak Arabic with them. My mother also spoke Arabic, and in the market place, most of the vendors were Arabs. The relationships between the Arabs and Jews were very friendly. We had an Arab gardener who would come once a week to clean and take care of the yard. At the marketplace, my mother would haggle over the price of the produce, all in Arabic. I used to speak Arabic as well, but forgot most of it.

Back in Our Neighborhood Elementary School

Once home, I was again to change schools at our neighborhood Tel-Nordoi elementary school on Frishman Street. Living with my mother brought many restrictions; the most difficult one was that I was not allowed to visit my father. This was a very painful restriction for me. I loved my father and missed seeing him, but now my mother was restricting me from seeing him. I guess she wanted to punish him for the 3½ years he kept us, and having to go to court to fight to gain custody of us. She had no idea how much she hurt me by this restriction, but she was consumed by anger against him and completely oblivious to my feelings. I occasionally sneaked out and visited him, which made me feel like a thief breaking the law. I could not do that too often, and therefore did not get to visit my father as much as I would have liked to.

Sometimes, my mother would find out that I went to visit him when a neighbor would tell her that they saw me in the vicinity where my father lived. She would be very angry with me and give me the silent treatment, which she often did when I did not obey her. The silent treatment would last for about a week or sometimes longer. You could cut the silence with a knife, and the energy she created was so unbearable. Unfortunately, this pattern repeated itself, as I had a hard time accepting or agreeing with her views and opinions. It went against my grain. I was very much my own person from a very young age and very different from her.

Difficult Time Adjusting to Our Neighborhood School

Back at Tel-Nordoi School, in third grade again, it was very hard for me. I did so well at the Alliance School and enjoyed it so much, and now I had to start all over again in a new environment with kids that had no care in the world except to do well and enjoy playing at recess time.

I was ill at ease in class, and didn't feel prepared for the subjects we were studying. When the teacher would call on me by saying "Turgeman" (we were called by our last name), it would send a shivering feeling down my spine and into the pit of my stomach.

I managed to be a fair student. The teacher knew I could do better and thought I was not applying myself. She had no idea of my inner turmoil. Math was a subject I could not comprehend at all. It was as if I had a mental block when it came to that subject. I managed to get Ds in Math and in other subjects I was a C and B student. Gymnastics was my favorite subject and I was very good at it; I was an A student in Gymnastics. During intermission I began to play with my classmates in the schoolyard; and eventually I managed to enjoy the intermission time.

When school ended at 3:00 p.m., I would stop on the way home for an hour to watch through a window a ballet dance class at the Gertrude Kraus Dance Studio, which was on our street. I wanted so much to take dance lessons or learn to play a musical instrument, but my mother could not afford the lessons, nor did she have a feeling for the arts like I did.

(As I am writing and recollecting these times, tears begin flowing. I feel so much for this little girl who wanted to do so much, but circumstances did not permit her to have these experiences.)

Our Street and Neighborhood

The street we lived on was full of cultured people: artists, actors, musicians, comedians, and painters. It was called the Habimah Compound. Habimah is the Israeli National Theater. It was established in Moscow in 1918 and re-established in Israel/Palestine in 1936.

All the artists and actors built homes next to one another, beginning with the house next to ours. Our house was 23 Frug Street and starting with number 25 to the end of the street at number 33 lived all the Habimah actors and musicians, continuing around the corner to Gordon Street and around to Dov-Hoz Street. Some of the famous actors—like Meskin, Klatchkin, and Hanna Rovina, who were stars of the Israeli National Theater—along with others, were all our neighbors.

It was like having Broadway actors as your neighbors, seeing them on a daily basis as they go about their business between their theatrical , daily shopping, and chores. There were no limousines driving by, distances were very short, and people did a lot of walking; cars were few and far between.

In the house next to ours on the second floor lived Mr. Fordhouse, who was the conductor for the Habimah Orchestra. The Fordhouse's had two daughters, Shula and Puah. Shula played the violin and Pouah the piano. They would practice their music daily for hours and I enjoyed absorbing the music by osmosis.

On the third floor lived Mr. and Mrs. Amitai. Mr. Amitai was a Habimah actor and his wife was a teacher. The Amitai's had two sons, Moshe and Noach. They were also studying to play musical instruments. Noach played the violin while Moshe played the cello. They would practice daily for hours. Thanks to this environment, I know by heart many classical symphonies and love listening to music.

The houses were very close to one another. We all kept our windows open for fresh air, and you could almost hear every conversation going on if they spoke loudly. We would chat with our neighbors through the balconies or open windows on occasion.

The daylight basement of this building next to ours was used as a rehearsal hall for plays that were planned to open at the Habimah Theater. I would sit at our third floor window mesmerized by viewing and listening to the rehearsals taking place. I could totally lose myself by listening and watching all the art adjacent to my home but not in my home. I was so lucky to have all this around me. It was a great escape from my reality, and a great cultural exposure.

My sister was kind of a tomboy and liked to tease me. She knew I could not handle sad and gory stories, so she would make up the most horrible sad and gory stories to tell me. I would run away from her while putting my hands over my ears to avoid hearing her, but she would run after me, pull my hands away from my ears, and would continue with the gory details of her made-up stories. It was quite cruel of her. I would envision what she was telling me, and it touched my heart to hear about people getting hurt. She would make up stories of people in accidents and bleeding. I guess this was her way of interacting with me at the time.

1945 - My Sister Got Engaged

When I was 11½ and in the 7th grade, my sister got engaged. Her husband to be, Nat Goldstein/Grant, was in the Royal British Air Force and living in Cairo, Egypt. His brother, Albert Goldstein, who was a captain in the British Royal Army, was married to our cousin, Alice Moyal-Goldstein. Nat came over for Passover to visit his brother. He saw my sister and fell madly in love with her. After his short visit, he returned to Egypt and sent my sister at least 5 letters and cards daily, pouring his love for her in his beautiful handwriting.

Although my sister was not in love with Nat, she was swept off her feet by all that attention and the opportunity to get out of our mother's house. Nat proposed, and at age 17 and Nat at 24, they got married. After the wedding they left for Cairo, Egypt where he lived with his mother.

1946 - My Security Blanket, Ruthie, Leaves

I was 12 when my sister left for Egypt with her husband. This was a devastating experience for me. It felt as if my whole world came to an end. What was I to do without my sister, who was my only sense of security in this world? I felt alone and unprotected.

I was unable to concentrate on my schoolwork any longer. I was unable to play with my classmates at intermission. During intermission, I would stand in the corridor, hiding behind the classroom door, and cry. During class I was unable to comprehend what was being taught. I was overcome with grief. I had no one to talk to but God and myself.

After a few months, as the end of the school year was approaching, I realized that my grades would fail me, and I would have to repeat the 7th grade again. This was not something I was prepared to face. I decided I would drop out of school and go get a job.

I could not see any other option for me at that time and having no one to consult with, I knew this was what I had to do. I could no longer see myself in a school environment with happy children my age; I had to change my environment. I decided I wanted to go to work and be around adults I could trust, respect, and emulate.

No one could sway me from my decision. My mother tried, and so did her friends, my teacher, and even the school principal took the time to talk me out of my decision to quit school. They all said I will regret it one day, but their words rang hollow for me. I knew what I wanted and had to do.

At that time, there was no mandatory law of minimum schooling required for children—this law was enacted a few years later—and I had already made my move.

My Work Experience

The work place and life became my school. I wanted to be around adults I could trust, respect, and emulate. I was very quiet and observant at work. I was eager to do my best on a job and to learn a craft.

My first job was as a seamstress apprentice. I applied when I saw a sign in the window "looking for seamstress apprentice." I walked in and presented myself as a 15-year-old girl looking to become a seamstress apprentice. I was only 12 at the time, but looked older than my age. I was hired. The hours were from 8:00 a.m to 1:00 p.m. and from 3:00 to 6:00 p.m. In Israel, most shops close between 1 to 3 p.m. for a siesta and at 7:00 p.m. for the day. The work week was Sunday to Friday, 6 days a week. Work was my refuge.

The first salon I applied to was a very exclusive high end seamstress salon and quite an expensive one, too. The clientele were wealthy and elegant ladies. It was, however, a small place, with just the seamstress and me the apprentice. I was very dependable and a fast learner. I seemed to have a good hand for sewing. The seamstress predicted that I had a big future in this line of work due to the talent she saw in me. I was taught by the seamstress the basics: how to tie a knot at the end of the thread, how to sew an invisible stitch to finish a hem, and how to finish a garment on the inside so that the fabric wouldn't fray, and also how to use a thimble. I was proud of the fact that my work was good and I was appreciated and liked.

I gave my mother most of the salary I earned and kept a bit for myself to buy clothes. I liked having nice clothes and I looked well in nice clothes.

After about six months at that first work place I decided to switch to a larger salon with more people working there, I felt a need to be around more people. I did my work while observing people's behavior silently. This next salon I applied to was a dress shop with a street front and in the back were the seamstresses creating the dresses and fitting dresses for clients. There were five operators and two apprentices of which I was one. This was on Dizengoff Street, which was just two blocks from my house.

During this time, a war was going on. Palestine was under British occupation and there was barbed wire at certain checkpoints to check identity cards. The British were looking for terrorists who undermined their rule. I looked a few years older than I was, and at checkpoints, the British would ask to see my identity card. I liked looking older than I was and was proud they asked for my identity and considered me to be an adult.

Rationing of Food and Clothes during the War

In early 1950, an austerity program was implemented. There was shortage of everything due to the war, and the government imposed a rationing on food and clothing. A coupon book was given to every family, and depending on the size of the family, was the amount of coupons you would get for food, clothes, and shoes.

Mothers learned how to do with less. We would get a quarter-pound of butter once a month. Eggs, flour, and all other food items were rationed. You could buy one pair of shoes per season, and once you used your coupons, you could not get the items you needed until the next month or several months later. However, we managed to survive. This time was more difficult for the parents than for the children. Parents had to be very creative in meal planning and clothes buying.

The British Occupation and the Quota Imposed

The British captured the land from the Turks during World War I. They imposed immigration restrictions and only allowed a limited number of Jewish refugees to enter the country legally, both before WWII and after. This resulted in a massive illegal immigration.

Over 100,000 people attempted to illegally enter Palestine between the years 1934–1948. Some succeeded, but many perished. (Much historical documentation online and in books is available on that cruel period for the Jews in Europe.) Boats with immigrants fleeing the concentration camps to come to the Promised Land were arriving at the shores of Tel Aviv, Jaffa, Acre, and Haifa.

The Jewish underground were busy helping the immigrants escape the British quota; the British wanted to deport them back to where they came from. The underground knew when the boats would arrive and were prepared to help the refugees quickly vanish before the British would be aware that a boat had arrived. Many homes were open to hide the refugees until they could be integrated into the country.

I remember one morning going to the beach (we lived about a five-minute walk from the beach) and seeing the refugee ship, Altalena, docked at the shore of Tel Aviv, just between Frishman and Gordon Streets. As I was walking up Frishman Street to the beach, I encountered fleeing refugees. They entered homes that welcomed and hid them from the British. They were given identities, jobs, and absorbed into the community. They were saved from the strong, politically incorrect, and cruel arm of the British.

Another time, I remember hearing an air raid when I was at work. A siren would blast the air telling people to go to shelter and empty the streets. The salon I was working at was on the ground floor, so we remained in place and continued working. Suddenly, a bomb fell next door. Fragments from the bomb hit our place of work. A gush of water filled the room from a water pipe explosion. A bomb fragment hit a pregnant co-worker sitting next to me and she later died of her injuries.

The impact of the bomb is something I can feel today as I recall it. The feeling is hard to describe; it shakes you to the core of your being. As soon as this happened, I instinctively ran home through the deserted streets while the air raid was still active.

I lived just two blocks from work. When I reached my home, all the neighbors were still sitting in the shelter waiting for the siren to sound that all was clear and we could resume whatever we were doing. I came in totally out of breath and unable to utter a word, I tried to tell what I had just experienced, but I could not make a sound. I was in shock. My mother and the neighbors tried to revive me with water. It took quite a while before I was able to speak and relate my experience.

The British on occasion, conducted house-to-house searches. They were looking for hidden ammunition and underground connections of citizens to terrorist activities. I remember our house being searched. They went through everything with a fine toothed comb. We felt violated as they went through all our linens, clothes closet, and everywhere they thought ammunition could be hidden. They did not find anything at our house.

My Father Got Married

In 1945, my father got married to a nice woman from Syria. Her name was Adel. Adel was a tall, slender lady with dark black hair pulled back, small dark eyes, and a very sweet disposition. She was a good wife to our father. A year later, their first daughter, Nava, was born. I would visit occasionally when I could. Adel was a good-natured woman, and I liked her. Every year for my birthday she would bake me homemade baklava. This is a delicious Middle Eastern desert made with phyllo dough, butter, honey, and almonds. I loved food and especially the baklava she made for me.

Several years later, they had a son named Eli. His nickname was Kiko. My father was so happy to have a son. Kiko was very bright and a delightful boy. Unfortunately, around the age of eleven he got ill. At first they did not know what the illness was, it was later diagnosed he had Cushing Syndrome, which affects the pituitary glands. A short while after his Bar Mitzvah, Kiko passed away. I was in the United States already and was not aware of the hardship they went through with his illness.

Kiko passed away after my father did, which was a blessing in a way. My father did not have to experience the death of his only son. However, his wife Adel did and I am sure it was very difficult time for her.

1947 - Changing Professions (Age 13)

I decided that being a seamstress was not my calling. I wanted more interaction with people. As a seamstress, the interaction is more with the fabric than with people. I decided to apply to a beauty salon as a hairdresser apprentice. When walking on Ben Yehuda Street, I passed by a hairdresser salon and saw an ad in the window, "Looking for an apprentice." I applied and was hired as an apprentice. It was called Salon Sarah and it was five blocks walk from my home. They had five operators and one manicurist, plus the owner, Sarah, and her husband, Shimon. I was the first apprentice there. My job was to sweep the floors after a haircut, shampoo the customers' hair, make sure the towels were hung to dry, remove curlers and get the customers ready for the stylist. I enjoyed this place.

The women hairstylists were mostly from Europe and had migrated to Palestine as refugees. Some had escaped from concentration camps and had numbers tattooed on their arms. They were intelligent, educated, kind, and decent human beings, and I liked their human qualities. They were different from what I had been exposed to in my family. It felt good going to work. They also liked my work ethics and appreciated me.

I learned the craft by observing, I was not taught directly how to cut hair or how to style. It took about nine months for me to absorb the craft and I began to take care of new customers who did not know I was just an apprentice. I would cut hair and style hair. I liked making the customer look good and I was good at it.

At fifteen, I realized that I must move on and build new clientele in a place that accept me as a hairdresser and not just an apprentice. I moved to another salon as a full-fledged hairdresser.

It was a small salon. The owner was from Persia, and I was hired as the only operator with him. I developed a loyal clientele who liked my work. Apparently I was talented at this craft. I enjoyed making women look good and I gave great hair cuts.

The new salon I moved to was much further from home. It was in the south part of town and I would ride there on my bicycle. I made new friends who did not know that I was a school dropout. They knew me as a talented hairdresser and they liked me.

Two of the friends had motorcycles with a sidecar and a group of us would travel the countryside and have a fun time on weekends. Israelis have a love relationship with their land, and therefore, love to travel the countryside, which is quite beautiful and versatile. It is different in its topography from the south to the north and from the east to the west, and yet it's not too far to travel for the day due to its small territory.

The whole state of Israel is smaller than the size of New Jersey. Israel has only one river, the Jordan River. The total size of Israel is 8,000 square miles. It is 263 miles long from north to south and 71 miles wide from east to west.

Israel is surrounded by Arab nations and Iran. These countries outnumber Israel's territory by more than 650 to 1 in terms of land and approximately 60 to 1 in terms of population. With all this, they just want the small territory of Israel for their Palestinians who should have been absorbed and made citizens of their Arab countries, instead of keeping them all these years as political pawns living in tents all their life and without a home. Israel absorbed all the refugees who came from the diaspora into its tiny country. So why didn't the Arabs absorb their people? Obviously, because they served their politicians agenda.

Back to my life... I dated a young man named Yossi for a short while. His father owned a candy factory. The factory was around the corner from the beauty salon I was working at, and that's how we met. He worked for his father, was quite well off, and he liked me very much. I liked him as a friend, but was not attracted to him romantically. Yossi wanted to marry me, but I was not interested, so the friendship ended.

When I was still at Salon Sarah, people thought I was seventeen. Every Saturday I would meet with friends and we would go to the beach walking the promenade and meeting with more friends. I pretended to be older than I was, and most people I met did not know my background.

Falling in Love for the First Time

My first love was at age sixteen when I met Ernest Weiss. Ernest was very handsome, tall, blonde with blue eyes, charming, a great dancer, and was a few years older than I. He had immigrated to Palestine from Romania with his parents. His father's business was manufacturing buttons, and he worked with his father. Most people in Israel at the time had personal seamstress or a tailor to sew clothes for them. Manufacturing buttons for clothes was a good business to be in.

We were in a group of about six couples who were all good friends, and we would go ballroom dancing every Saturday night. On Friday evenings we would have a party at someone's home, or we would play cards. On Saturday mornings we would meet at the same spot on the beach, play racketball, swim, and visit with each other. These were good and fun times.

Ernest and I dated for about a year. One day I was told by one of our mutual friends that Ernest and his family had immigrated to Argentina. I was in shock. Why did he not tell me that he was leaving? I was told that he could not deal with the separation and the pain, so he decided to ask our friend to tell me instead.

He later wrote to me and we corresponded for quite a while. I cried after he left for quite some time. He was a good dancer, a good friend, and a kind person. He was also a great kisser. We loved to cuddle and kiss, I could lose myself kissing. It felt so good. We did not have sex, as I was too young and very naive.

He wrote to me after he arrived in Argentina and we corresponded in English since his Hebrew was not very good. I remember he would sign his letters, "Yours with all my love and soul, Ernest." I did not know what the word soul meant, as it was the first time I encountered it. I asked a friend what it meant, and was very happy to find out it's meaning.

As time is a healer, I finally got over the heartache of missing Ernest. Our correspondence helped me in mastering the English language. I am glad he came into my life when he did. This was, however, a second experience of being abandoned by someone I loved and trusted. (First was my sister leaving and now Ernst)

I was not aware at the time what effect this might have on my life and on the relationships that ensued. Now, at age 77 in Atlanta as I am writing my book, I sometimes wonder what became of him. I would love to go to Argentina and look him up, but this is unrealistic. I began to make new friends and move on with my life.

1948 - The State of Israel Was Born

On May 14, 1948, Israel declared its independence just as the British Mandate was terminated and the responsibility of maintaining a sovereign state was given to the Jewish State to be called Israel. A provisional government was created and the birth of Israel as an independent Jewish state became a reality. Israel was born. I remember that day and night so vividly.

Prior to that date, on 29 November 1947, the General Assembly of the UN adopted a resolution for the partition of Palestine into two states. That was the beginning of forcasting the creation of a home for the Jewish people.

Hatikvah, the Israeli anthem flowed through the radio as the UN proclaimed the birth of the State of Israel. We were dancing in the streets all night with joy; we now had a country and it was called Israel! The streets became a big celebration for all Israelis. The joy we felt was infectious;

it was as if we all became one. Unfortunately, our joy was soon replaced with a war for our survival.

The first undertaking by the Israeli new provisional government was to null and void the White Paper of 1939, written into law by the British Government. The White Paper restricted the immigration of Jews into the country and forbade the purchase of land by Jews in all but 5% of its areas. Palestine was almost the only country in the world in 1948, in which the law discriminated against immigrants and residents on the grounds of their being Jewish. This cruel law was applied when Jews were being slaughtered by the millions in Europe. The newly formed government of Israel opened the flood gates to immigration into Israel for those seeking a refuge in their homeland.

The Arab nations rejected the partitions voted by the United Nations and in a single voice declared war and suggested that Israel would not exist one month after its birth. Israel responded in defense for its survival and won that war but not the peace.

The Arabs that resided in Palestine at the time were told by their Arab leaders to leave their homes and escape, since a war was being waged against Israel. They were also told that within one month they would return to their homes after they won the war. The Arab nations were so sure they would win the war and claim Israel/Palestine for their own. The numbers were surely on their side. Egypt, Syria and Jordan, three armies with one purpose, tried to push Israel into the sea. Israel was surrounded by them, but Israel's survival instinct was stronger than the hatred of these armies determined to crush and drown her.

Had the Arabs accepted the partition mandated by the UN for two countries living side by side, the region would truly be "the land of milk and honey." Israelis and Arabs lived side by side in peace for centuries and were good neighbors to each other prior to the partition.

The Arabs that elected to remain and not flee are today Israeli citizens, and are given all the rights that Israelis have. They are full-fledged Israeli citizens. They have equal voting rights, and can serve in the Israeli Parliament.

After Israel won the war of independence, the Arab refugees who were told to flee, have since been used as political pawns by their corrupt Arab leaders. The Palestinian refugees could have easily been absorbed into their Arab countries, just like Israel absorbed the Jewish refugees from the diaspora. The Arab nations surely have much more land than the small territory of Israel. However, their corrupt politicians have kept the Palestinian refugees all these years living in tents, without a home or the benefit of belonging to a country, using their own people as political pawns, and indoctrinating them with hatred toward Israel and the Jews.

If achieving peace was in the peoples' hands, rather than politicians, I am sure we would have peace today, and we would all benefit. However, politicians have their own agenda, which does not take in consideration the peoples' well being.

The Jews and Muslims have more in common than they have differences. Peace would benefit everyone. Hatred only breeds more conflict, and the blame game benefits no one. I so wish for peace in the region to become a reality. From my mouth to God's ear—AMEN!

1949 - My Sister Is Back

My sister, along with her husband and their seven-month-old daughter Diana, fled Egypt as the war erupted. They came back to Israel, this time as refugees. My mother vacated an apartment on the ground floor of our house so that they would have a place of their own. My sister was so happy to be reunited with me, and I was glad to see her too, however I had moved on and built my own life since she left.

I did not have much time for her. She wanted me to babysit for her daughter, but I was not available to her. I was too busy with my own life. I had become a teenager. She was hurt and disappointed, I later found out. I was unaware of this at the time; I was too absorbed in the life I created for myself.

My brother-in-law, Nat, tried to make a living in Israel, but he did not speak Hebrew and this made it harder for him to find a suitable job. He got a job at a factory manufacturing false teeth. He worked there for three months and before he would become a permanent employee, he was fired. They did not want to have the obligation of him becoming a permanent employee, which would obligate them to give him better pay along with job compensations and benefits. He found this to be the case in other jobs he tried. It was a difficult time for them.

Since he had a British passport and was a British subject, they decided to immigrate to England where he had an older brother who was doing very well for himself. This older brother, Albert, was married to our first cousin, Alice.

My mother, my sister and I owned the house we lived in at 23 Frug Street. My sister asked my mother if she would help them monetarily so they could have a fresh start in England. Mother was not willing to help. I am not sure if she did not have the money or just refused to help. They were in a bind; life for them in Israel had no future.

My sister, with a help of a friend, rented the apartment secretly without my mother or I knowing anything about it. She received one year's rent in advance and that gave them the opportunity to start a new life in England. After they changed hands with the new tenants, they fled overnight and took a boat to London. We found out after the fact that my sister had left. My mother was livid and did not speak to her for several years.

1952 - Time to Enlist in the Army (Age 18)

Every Israeli at age eighteen has to enlist in the army for two years. At the time, when I was to enlist, there was a choice to either enlist in the army for two years or in the police force for three years with a full salary. I chose the police force. However, for them to accept me in the police force, I had to have office work skills, which I did not have.

I was a hairdresser, with no office or typing skills and a school drop out. My mother had a good friend in the police force, and he suggested I say that I worked for an attorney my mother knew. He said that I would be trained anyhow to whatever position I would be assigned to.

So, I lied on my application, gave the name of my mother's attorney as my employer, and was accepted to the police force. I was assigned to work at the police headquarters, in a department handling all the criminal files. My job was getting the files ready for court and filing the correspondence from the attorneys regarding each case.

I had to open the daily mail, read the letters find the correct file and case to include in the file, and cross-reference the correspondence so that the file was up-to-date and ready for court. I quickly learned my job well, and found it most interesting; I also liked the people I was working with.

I had an inside knowledge to famous criminal cases that were written about in the daily newspapers. Some cases were being dragged in the courts for years, and the files were very big and heavy. I enjoyed this line of work. I made some good friends at the police headquarters and loved my job.

Becoming an Immigration Officer at the Airport

After one and a half years at this position, halfway through my service, I heard that the airport police needed to fill a position for an immigration officer. I went to my superior and said that I would be interested in being transferred to the airport for the open position they had. He tried to persuade me against this move by saying that the hours were long and I'd be required to work weekends and holidays, as well as night shifts. I told him I didn't mind, so reluctantly, he recommended me for the move.

Since I was a young child, I had wanted to be an air hostess one day. This was my dream. Both of my cousins, Carmela and Helena Moyal, were air hostesses. In fact, Carmela was the very first air hostess hired by El Al. I remember admiring them as they travelled the world, and they looked so glamorous in their uniforms.

Moving to work at the airport, I thought, would bring me a step closer to my goal in spite of the fact that I did not have the required education.

My duties as an immigration officer were to process the passengers when flights came in. I would sit in a booth behind a window; next to me was a big book from the Interpol police. The book had names of wanted criminals internationally.

I was to check each visitor against that list, checking their passport information against the Interpol list and making sure they were not a wanted criminal. Once they were cleared, I would stamp their passport and move to the next passenger, and so on.

It helped that I spoke several languages. I spoke English, French, German, and of course, Hebrew. I was often asked by airline personnel to assist in expediting the checking of VIPs, which I gladly did. This helped me create a friendship with top management in El-Al, Israeli Airlines, as well as other airlines.

Working at the airport, a new family of good friends was created. Between the customs officers, the airline personnel, and the police immigration officers, we were all like one big happy family. It was like an international melting pot—some of the people were from Iraq some from Rumania, Germany, Yemen, Turkey, and Israel. What a wonderful cultural environment this was, and we all got along very well. We had respect for one another, and we were fond of one another. (I wish the world was that way.) We spent many a night sitting in the airport café, visiting with each other, and killing time, as we waited for flights to come in. There were not as many flights then as there are today, and Ben-Gurion Airport was very small compared to what it is today. There was a feeling of camaraderie between us all.

1953 - A New Beginning (Almost 20 Years Old)

The time had come; my three years of duty came to an end. I had a choice to continue working for the police if I wanted to, or to move on and apply for an airline position. My site was set on becoming an air hostess.

The airline had scheduled interviews for potential stewards and stewardesses. I was told this process was very demanding. You had to appear before a board of five airlines executives who would be interviewing you for this sought after position. There were more than a hundred applicants for only twelve spaces to fill.

I completed my application answering all the questions on it, and when it came to the question about my education, I had to lie. If I would tell the truth about my lack of formal education, I wouldn't have a chance to be considered.

Lucky for me, when my turn came to go in and be interviewed, all the airline executives knew me, and had no doubt about my qualifications. They surmised from knowing me that I had passed the required qualifications, the only problem they had with me was the fact that I was too young. I was only 20, and the minimum age was at 22. However, they said if all my other qualifications were in place they would hire me. The fact that I spoke several languages was in my favor. I was accepted to work for the airline. At first though, they started me as a ground hostess.

1954 - Hired By the Airlines (Age 20)

I worked as a ground hostess for about six months, and in the summer of 1954, I was assigned to attend a three weeks course for air hostesses and stewards. The course was from May 23, 1954 - June 13, 1954. There were 16 of us in this course, 5 men and 11 women, carefully chosen for this sought after position. This particular course we attended was never repeated. It was highly stressful on all of us, and one of the women had a nervous breakdown and was hospitalized.

We stayed in a dormitory setting where we shared a room with two to a room. We were watched as if we were under a microscope every moment of the day. They checked how we kept our room, made our bed, how we ate, and how we looked in the morning. During the day, we attended classes on the subjects of: Flight Attendants Duties, Flight Planning, Weather Routes, Aircraft Familiarization, First Aid, Emergency Procedures, and General Company Rules.

I had a hard time with some of the geography and math needed for some of the subjects, but somehow I managed to complete the course and graduate. Some of the answers I gave on the tests were a good guess rather than based on my understanding of the question.

I Am Now an Air Hostess

I became a full-fledged air hostess. My dream was accomplished. We were first scheduled to meet with the airlines tailor; the uniforms were made to measure for each one of us. We got two skirts, two jackets, several white shirts, and a hat. We were also issued a crew tag to put on our luggage. I still sometimes have a recurring dream that I am scheduled to go on a flight, and my skirt is soiled and I am trying to hide it.

The routes we would fly were between Israel, Istanbul, Rome, Vienna, Zurich, Paris, London, New York, and Johannesburg. In Johannesburg I had a boyfriend by the name of Mike; we would date when my flight would bring me there. I was appalled, however, by the way the South Africans treated their servants. I could not stomach their treatment. They had separate elevators for black and white Africans. I could not see myself living there with these conditions, so our friendship was short lived.

On longer flights, we would have several days layover. We flew a C-46 plane on shorter routes, and the Constellation on longer flights. This was before the jet age, and flights took much longer to reach their destination.

Flying around the world was exciting. I enjoyed being of service to the passengers, as well as taking care of the cockpit crew. Because the flights were longer, there was much time left for connecting and chatting with passengers between food services. It happened frequently on flights from New York that passengers wanted to introduce me to their Jewish sons; I would just smile, and move on to another passenger.

I enjoyed talking to the passengers, and could change languages as needed, from Hebrew to French to German and English. Switching languages came very easy to me. I didn't have to pause in order to think in another language it just came naturally. I must have been a gifted linguist.

I had a romantic relationship with a Captain GK. He was as cute as can be, and we had a good time when we were scheduled to fly together. We would go to the theater or to dinner in exotic places. I also dated a flight engineer for a short while, but it was not a good match.

The movie actor, Danny Kaye, was on one of my flights, and he wanted me to teach him a Hebrew song. I taught him *Hava Nagila,* which translates as "let's be merry." He was very funny, but also very demanding of my time, and he was also quite self-centered. He came to Israel to attend the premiere of his movie, *Jacobovsky and the Colonel.* I was invited by him to attend and was given two tickets for this gala occasion.

I had a poodle named ChiCha. ChiCha sensed when I would return from a flight. When the crew car was at the end of our street, she would stand by the window and bark, while wagging her tail with joy knowing I would be home soon.

I also enjoyed the fact that I could shop for pretty clothes in London and New York. I was one of the best dressed in Tel-Aviv. I brought clothes and gifts for my mother and for my friends as well. Flying gave me the opportunity to buy things that were either not available in Israel or were extremely expensive. We had to declare to customs if we purchased a camera, or an expensive item, and it would be recorded in our passport.

Some of the crew members thought that because I used to be an immigration officer, I would spy on them and report if they did not declare an item they purchased. This was furthest from my thinking, but they probably had a guilty conscience and assumed that I would tell. It took me a while to gain their confidence and not feel alienated by some of the crew members.

I recall that in most of my relationships with boyfriends and friends, I spoke very little about myself. I felt insecure. I also felt inferior, and I covered this feeling by concentrating on my friends' issues and interests. I was also sarcastic in my interactions; it made me feel wise and powerful in responding during conversations with people. As I matured, I realized that being sarcastic was not a good way to communicate and I nixed that aspect of my personality.

I realized that people liked to talk about themselves, and by my showing an interest in them, they considered me intelligent. I thought I discovered the formula for gaining friends and influencing people! It was sincere however; I could not act in an insincere manner. This was the way I covered up for my insecure feelings.

It took me many years into my adulthood to own up to the fact that although I lacked formal schooling, I was knowledgeable and intelligent. A degree does not make a person intelligent; it just gives knowledge. Life was my school, and I was and still am an avid student of life.

I feel fortunate for having been born in Israel. People are very warm, hospitable, and friendly. You always feel welcome at people's homes. You can just drop in to visit friends without needing an invitation. Israelis are very honest, and you rarely have a superficial relationship. Life is too short for a superficial front; you might as well be frank and know who your friends are. Growing up in this kind of environment made it easier to endure the difficulties I had at home.

Distances are very short in Tel Aviv, and I would do a lot of walking. On the way to wherever I went, I could always stop by for a visit with friends. It was a very positive environment to grow up in. Friends were always happy to see me, and refreshments were always provided. It was either home-baked cakes or Middle Eastern fare such as hummus, pita bread, olives, and cheese. There might also be a wonderful Israeli salad, which consists of cucumbers, tomatoes, parsley cut into small pieces, and a dressing of just olive oil, salt, pepper, and fresh lemon juice. My mouth is drooling now as I remember how good and tasty it was.

My favorite place to be was always at the beach. The Mediterranean Sea was so beautiful, the water so blue and inviting, the sand so soft, almost like talcum powder and watching the sunset was absolutely breathtaking in its beauty; the sky turns orange and red as the sun, looking like a big red ball, slowly sets behind the horizon. When the sea is calm, it looks like a blue plate of glass, so peaceful and beautiful.

Due to the immigration of Jews from Eastern Europe and the diaspora, I was exposed to many different cultures and languages. We had neighbors that spoke Hungarian, German, English, French, Russian, Polish, and Yiddish. Israel was a melting pot, it was a great place to be, and the exposure to the different cultures was an education in itself.

New York Friends and Relatives

I had friends in New York, and we would go to the theater, which I enjoyed very much. Also, in London I would visit my sister and go to the theater whenever I could.

I remember my first visit to New York; I could not get over the large portion sizes of food and deserts given at restaurants. Having experienced the rationing of food during the war, it seemed to me like such a waste of food, and I thought, "Who could eat so much?"

I also had cousins in New York, and I loved visiting them. They owned a very prestigious antique firm called, "Israel Sack Antiques," specializing in early American antiques. Their show room was on 57th Street near Madison Avenue. They were my second cousins. Their father, Israel Sack, was my mother's uncle, but he was no longer alive when I met them. All three brothers, Harold, Albert, and

Robert, were partners in the antique business that their father had created.

My favorite cousin was Harold. Harold's wife was Loretta, and they had four sons: Kenneth, David, Michael, and Danny. They were a very warm and loving family, and Loretta was very sweet and hospitable. Later in life, when I lived in New York and was married to George, we used to visit them, and on Thanksgiving and Passover we were always guests in their home. Loretta was a good cook, and during big family dinners she would have a helper to serve and clean the dishes. Their home had mainly American antique furniture and the dishes were elegant, with very nice silverware. They lived in Oceanside, Long Island in a two story unpretentious house with a basement, where all the children were brought up, and later, the grandchildren would make it their home while visiting. It was a very warm home with much love.

Harold Sack wrote a book about American antiques titled, *American Treasure Hunt, The Legacy of Israel Sack*. His book was published in 1986. If you ever want to learn about American antiques and its history, I highly recommend the book. (ISBN 0-316-76593-7)

Harold signed his book for me and wrote: "To Miki, Your courage and outstanding ability in human relations is a joy to behold, Affectionally, Cousin Harold."

They were members in a private beach club with a cabana. On one of my flights to New York, I was invited to go with them to their private beach club. I remember wearing a bikini bathing suit. It created such a commotion, as they had never seen anyone wearing a bikini before. My cousin Harold enjoyed the shock on his neighbors' faces. I had no idea I did anything wrong. Apparently bikinis were not allowed at this private beach club. I broke the rule. So what else was new?

There was always plenty of food at their cabana. They had a small refrigerator in the cabana, and it was equipped with lots of fruits, salads, bread, and cold cuts for sandwiches, it was always like a feast, so very nice and warm.

My mother's younger sister, Bella, lived in New Jersey, and my cousin Robert took me to meet her. She was such a delightful person, sweet, intelligent, and sensitive. She resembled my mother, and even their voices sounded alike. Bella and her husband Kal Lind had a young son Bernie. Bernie was about twelve years old when I first met her.

I would visit Bella when my flight would bring me to New York. Unfortunately, Bella died a short while after I met her, and I lost contact with her son Bernie for many years. Bernie, years later, made a trip to Israel and looked up my mother by following the address he had from my mothers' correspondence with his mother. He rang the doorbell at my mother's apartment, not knowing if she still lived there. My mother opened the door, and he was shocked to find the strong resemblance my mother had to his mother, Bella. It was a great reunion. Bernie, my sister, and I maintain contact with each other.

1952 and Beyond - Boyfriends

When I was still in the police force, I dated Benz Heiber who lived on the south end of our street. Benz looked a lot like the movie actor, Van Johnson; he was fair skinned, about 5′ 4″ with pretty blue eyes. We dated for about a year and we were engaged to be married. Just before setting a wedding date, I got cold feet. I realized that my reason for getting married did not justify getting married. I saw this as an escape from home, and I concluded that escaping from home was not a good enough reason to get married.

I remember the day I told Benz that I am breaking off with him. He was so in love with me, and it broke his heart, the poor man. He left my home crying. I felt bad for him, but felt good for making that crucial decision for my own good.

Benz got married shortly after our break-up, but he never got over his love for me. Years later, when I got married and lived in New York, and my mother was on her own, he acted like a son to her, often visited her to check if she needed anything, and always asked how I was doing. He wrote me several love letters. I did not respond to them, but was glad that he was caring for my mother. He kept the relationship with my mother until her death on December 1998.

I later had another boyfriend for about one year, Nani Gustin. He was the brother of the famous Israeli singer Yaffa Yarkoni. He was a very sweet and sensitive guy and I loved him. He had a deep sexy velvety voice and had deep dark eyes—you could almost see his soul through them. He was a musician and his family had a club outside Tel-Aviv, where they lived. He would always send me flowers when I would return from a flight with a note telling me how much he missed me while I was gone. We would always go out with a group of friends, one of whom was the journalist Uri Dan. Uri always went with us wherever we went. I later found out that Uri wanted to date me.

Love Betrayal Again

One day, I found out via Uri that Nani and his family immigrated to Argentina. Here again, I was told he could not deal with the breakup, and asked our friend to tell me. I was broken-hearted again, and I felt betrayed and abandoned by love. Uri Dan was waiting in the wings, hoping that now I would become his girlfriend. But I liked him as a friend, not a boyfriend. I later found out that Nani's family had many debts they could not handle, and that's why they escaped to Argentina. I never heard from

Nani again. I did find out from his sister Yaffa Yarkoni that he got married there and had several daughters.

My Sister in London - Visits

I would visit my sister, Ruth, in London whenever I had a stopover. By then, she had two daughters, Diana and Poppie. I enjoyed my visits, but I did not get along well with my brother-in-law. I did not trust him and we never saw eye-to-eye on anything. I know he felt that I could see through him. He was very domineering and demanding of my sister and expected a lot from her. He had to have a four-course dinner every night, which my sister provided. He made all the decisions, small and big, regarding the family without any input or consideration for my sisters' views.

At seventeen, my sister was too young to be married. She didn't have a chance to develop into an adult yet, and she was quite insecure and childlike. She was very beautiful, and her outer beauty was the extent of her focus. She was short, 5-feet tall, with a beautiful figure, a radiating smile exposing her beautiful pearl-like teeth, green eyes, and auburn color hair. She was simply gorgeous, and she was also a tomboy. A very sad event happened at a time when I visited them. Ruthie was forced by circumstances to find her inner beauty. (I will write about this later)

Life went on, and I continued flying and living at home with my mother. My relationship with her had not changed. I had some free time between flights, and used it by enrolling in a ceramics course. I enjoyed working with clay and completely immersed myself in the sculpture I was working on. I created some very nice pieces including some vases and a nude. I kept the pieces I created and still have them with me today.

As a hostess, I earned a nice salary, and instead of putting my savings in the bank I frequented art galleries and invested my money in paintings. At one point, when in New York and short of money, I sold two of my paintings by famous Israeli artists, Mokadi and Yosl Bergner. It helped me bridge a financial gap at the time. I still enjoy the rest of the paintings I purchased, and they are decorating the walls of my home today. I was drawn to paintings that portrayed sadness. My inner self identified with the suffering portrayed in the painting. I think that today I would probably purchase happier scenes in paintings. However, I still like the paintings I purchased at the time.

Mother's Silent Treatment and Needing Her Love

I remember one time when my mother was angry with me for something, and she gave me her silent treatment. I felt as if she did not love me or care about me.

I left on a flight for New York with a heavy heart. We used to stay at the Henry Hudson Hotel on 57th street, just behind the New York Coliseum.

It was a rainy wintry night when I entered my hotel room. I opened the window, sat beside it and started crying. My wish was to get deathly sick to see if my mother cared about me. In the morning I developed a high fever. I called the airline doctor and he diagnosed my condition as having pneumonia and checked me into the hospital. In addition to the pneumonia, I also developed the measles.

I was very sick, and stayed in the hospital for more than a week. The room had to remain dark due to the measles. I felt very alone, although the hospital took good care of me. When I returned home, my mother's behavior had not changed, although she did speak to me.

This incident shows how powerful our mind is. I wished to get very sick, and I managed to create it for real. However, it did not reveal to me what I wished to know, if my mother loved me.

In hindsight, I can forgive my mother for her harshness. She came from a very cruel childhood herself, and having a roof over our head and having food to eat was her way of showing love. She did not know any better. This is my conclusion.

1956 – The Sinai Campaign – My Shoes Made History (22 Years Old)

In 1956, there was a war called The Sinai Campaign. This war does not have the same place in the memory of the world as the wars of 1948 and 1967 do. This war was to ensure that Israel would not be cut out of the use of the Suez Canal and to eliminate the harassment from Gaza terrorists.

The establishment of a joint High Command to control the Egyptian, Syrian, and Jordanian armies left Israel no choice but to take swift action. This joining of arms was created on October 25, 1956.

This campaign began on October 29th, when the Israeli army forces under General Moshe Dayan burst into Sinai and Gaza with the intent of securing the freedom of its shipping lines through the straits of Tiran and to eliminate Gaza as a source of frontier harassment. It caught the Egyptian army by surprise and little resistance

was encountered while capturing the Gulf of Aqaba as they overran the Egyptian positions at Sharm-el-Sheik and opened the Red Sea to Israel.

By November 5th, this operation was over. Israel was buzzing with international press at the time and a cease-fire was declared. The next day, I received a telegram from the airline to be ready for a flight within Israel. I surmised that it would probably be a flight over Israel for the press. Usually, I would wear high-heel shoes with a pointed toe, which was the fashion at the time, and I would have a flat pair of shoes to change on the plane. This time, thinking it would be a short flight over Israel, I didn't bother to take a pair of flat shoes to change. Little did I know where we would end up.

The crew car arrived early in the morning to pick me up; the rest of the crew was already in the car. We were all in the dark as to where we were going or to which airport. We finally arrived at a military airport. As we exited the car, we were engulfed by a smoke screen as we boarded the aircraft which was a C46 twin engine.

Once on board the aircraft, it was revealed that we would be flying to the Sinai Desert, and our passengers would be Ben Gurion, the Prime Minister of Israel, with his wife, Paula, and daughter, Renana, Moshe Dayan, the Chief of Staff, and several high-ranking army officers.

The purpose of the flight was to view the captured territory and thank the soldiers for their service to the country. No wonder this flight was a secret. Had this plane been shot down, it would have taken all of Israel's leaders at one swoop. In hindsight, it was foolish to have Israel's entire leaders in one plane. But Israelis are bold and fearless.

During the flight, I was chatting with Moshe Dayan who was a womanizer, and he flirted with me and asked me for a date. I had a boyfriend at the time and told him he could join us, but he said he did not like to be the third wheel.

We arrived at Sharm-El-Sheik, and we all walked on the sandy desert to visit the soldiers and the territory captured. I walked in front with Ben Gurion, Moshe Dayan and Paula. Paula asked me how I could walk in the desert with such high heels. I told her I had no idea we would end up in the Sinai Desert.

We climbed on a tower to see the view. Sharm El Sheik is beautiful, and we predicted that this could be a wonderful resort town. Today, Mubarak has one of his palaces there. And it is indeed a beautiful and luxurious resort town.

We encountered much debris, such as helmets, shoes, and uniform parts left by the fleeing Egyptian soldiers.

My shoes made history. I was the first woman to walk the Sinai Desert in spike-heeled shoes.

July 1958 – Mexican Vacation (Age 24)

I had earned a two-week vacation from the airline. Being the trailblazer that I was, I decided to fly to Mexico City. None of our crew members ever took a vacation to Mexico, and for some reason I decided that's where I wanted to go.

I had a free flight to New York City, and El Al had reciprocal relations with Flying Tigers, a freighter airline. I was booked on Flying Tigers out of New York to Los Angeles, and from there to Mexico City. Now, it seemed like a complicated routing. However, this was the routing arranged for me by the airline.

Since Flying Tigers was a freighter airline, there were no comfortable passenger seats on board, and I sat on a jump seat like a crewmember. The crew was very friendly, and one of the crewmembers, Jim, became a good friend of mine. We met several times in Paris when our flights co-in sided. We went to the Eifel Tower and did some touring in Paris. It was a very romantic time for both of us, which we cherished. However, Jim was a married man, and although we were drawn to each other, we acted responsibly and decided, as painful as it was, not to see each other and to respect his marriage.

On the way to Los Angeles we developed engine trouble and had to land in Las Vegas, instead of Los Angeles. We spent the night in Las Vegas. I played the slot machines for the first time in my life and won a jackpot of $100. It was very exciting. Another crew took over that plane, and we drove by car to Los Angeles. I parted from my new friends, and took a flight to Mexico City.

The Israeli Ambassador to Mexico was informed by the airline that an El Al stewardess was on her way to Mexico City. Since they had never had an Israeli stewardess visit Mexico, I was treated like a celebrity.

The ambassador arranged for a limousine and a driver to pick me up at the airport, and made hotel reservations for me. He scheduled a dinner at the Embassy in my honor, and invited five of Mexico City's most eligible Jewish bachelors. I felt like a star. The conversation at the table evolved around me, and the fact that I was born in Israel, and these young Jewish Mexican bachelors had never met an Israeli-born person. I have pictures with these five eligible bachelors dated July 8, 1958. They spoke very little English, and I could not speak Spanish; two of they're names were Joseph and Solomon. The next evening they took me to dinner and gave me a tour of Mexico City. I found Mexico City to be very colorful and interesting. They took me to the market place where I bought myself a big sombrero and a pair of maracas. The market was full of Mexican-made clothes, hats, musical instruments, and souvenirs. They showed me the residential area where they lived; it was quite luxurious and beautiful. They also took me to see the poor area, and I was left with the impression that there was no middle class there. It was either very wealthy or very poor.

Joseph, one of the five, also invited me to dinner the next evening; he spoke more English than his friends. He took me to one of Mexico's best restaurant, and I was wined and dined first class. The food was delicious and the atmosphere authentic Mexican, with the Mariachis strolling around the tables and playing their uplifting music. I loved the music and the undivided attention I received. We had a delightful evening. He was one of the wealthy elite of the Jewish community and he and his friends were seriously interested in marrying an Israeli girl, but I was not interested in marrying any of them. (Show 2 pictures from that event) I later flew to Acapulco and stayed there for four days. I loved Acapulco with its beautiful scenery, and I stayed in a hotel near the famous high-diving location. The beauty was breathtaking and so unique, and I found Acapulco to be one of the most beautiful resort places I have seen. This was a vacation I would never forget.When I returned to Israel from this exciting vacation, some of the airline personnel decided to go to Mexico on their vacation too, but I was the first one opening this route. I still don't know what made me decide to go to Mexico. I just followed my gut feeling about most of my decisions. If it felt right, I would go for it. I welcomed new experiences and new places.

1960 - Lausanne Switzerland (Age 26)

A wealthy Jewish philanthropist from Lausanne, Switzerland, Mr. Albert Bozdogan came to Israel looking for connections. He wanted to open an Israeli Art Center in Lausanne. Because of my fluency in French, mutual friends introduced me to him. He invited me to come to Lausanne, visit with his family, and see if I was interested in handling this venture. I was excited about this opportunity. I loved art, and representing Israeli art in Switzerland was an exciting offer. We agreed that I would come and run the center for 6 months. Mr. Bozdogan rented a storefront space not too far from his place of business. He was the owner of an exclusive fur shop. He was a furrier by profession.

I proceeded to ask for a six months sabbatical from the airline in order to accept this offer. The airline granted me the sabbatical, and off I flew to Lausanne. Upon arrival, I rented a studio apartment, which had a balcony overlooking Lake Geneva. It was breathtakingly beautiful.

Israeli art was shipped to the store by selected artists. I handled the decorations and the placing of the art. We had hand-made ceramics, paintings, and other specialty hand-made art by Israeli artists. It was also to be an Israeli promotion and information center. It was not meant to be a moneymaker. He wanted to promote Israel. And I was selected to do this. We scheduled a gala opening on December 9, 1959. The center was called "Israel Art Premiere Center of Israeli Art in Europe." The Israeli Ambassador to Switzerland Mr. Joseph Linton was invited, as well as other dignitaries. The Swiss television came to film the opening as a newsworthy event. I was introduced by Mr. Bozdogan as the person in charge of this Israeli center. The event was publicized in the local newspapers, as well as in Israeli newspapers, and broadcast for Swiss television.

The cameramen for the Swiss television liked me, and the next day he came to the store and invited me out to lunch. His name was Roger Bauvard. He was charming, very tall and handsome. He looked a lot like the movie star, Charlton Heston. We enjoyed each other's company, and he began to come often to take me out to lunch. I grew very fond of him, and it seemed that he was in love with me. We would talk a lot in French, and also in English as his English was quite good. In time, a romance developed, and we were in love.

As our relationship progressed, he suddenly confessed that he was married, and according to him, stuck in a very unhappy marriage and in the process of getting a divorce. I believed everything he said, and our relationship was wonderful. However, whenever I asked how the divorce was coming along, he would say that his wife tried to commit suicide every time he brought up the subject, and that I should be patient for the time being.

The six months venture in Lausanne was coming to an end, and I was to return to Israel and resume my duties as a stewardess for El-Al. I said goodbye to Roger. We said that we will be together again soon, as Roger took me to the airport. We kept communicating after I left, and he asked me to come back soon. I returned home and back to flying

June 1961 - Resigning from El Al (Age 27)

Roger kept communicating with me, and told me how much he missed me, that he was working on the divorce, and he wanted to marry me. He asked me to come back to Lausanne and we would have a future together. I loved him, and believed what he was saying. So, after about six months of flying, I decided to resign and move to Lausanne to join Roger, and I believed that we would soon get married.

My mother and my friends told me not to go, and wait until he had his divorce, but I was stubborn as usual, and my mind was made up. So I resigned from El-Al in June of 1961. I was entitled to a free round-trip ticket on El Al, and I used that ticket to fly to Lausanne.

I rented an apartment, and Roger would come visit, and we'd go to lunch and spend time together; however, he always had to go back home. And the story about his wife trying to commit suicide repeated itself.

I looked for a job to earn a living and stay productive, and was hired by a company selling carbon paper to businesses. I didn't particularly enjoy this job, but it was something to do while I was waiting for Roger to get his divorce.

Almost a year went by, and I began to suspect that he would never get a divorce. So one day, I told Roger that I was leaving him and going to New York, and not to Tel Aviv. I could not face my mother or my friends who told me that this would be the outcome. I chose to start a new life in New York City, where I had a cousin I could stay with. I told Roger that I no longer want to hear from him as long as he was still married. Should he get his divorce, he could come to New York and join me there. And that was the end of my experience in Lausanne. I left for New York with a heavy heart. I never heard from Roger again, and I often wondered what became of him.

1963 - A New Beginning in New York (Age 29)

I stayed for a while at my cousin's apartment. She was divorced and had a place for me, which I appreciated very much. What was I to do now? I had a tourist visa, which did not permit me to work. I did have some money with me, but if I didn't replenish it with a job, it would soon evaporate. So I became a student. I enrolled in the Herzliah Hebrew Teachers Institute, and I studied as an evening student from January 1963 until June 1964, at which time I dropped out.

Being a student allowed me to work. I did enjoy the time and the subjects taught, which were Biblical in nature. We studied the prophets, Biblical law, new literature, history, grammar, music, and drama. I did quite well with As and Bs and a C in grammar. I also got a steady job as a babysitter for a woman who needed to return to work as a teacher after giving birth to a baby girl.

I took care of her baby daughter daily from 8:00 a.m. to 4:00 p.m. I didn't have high expenses, and I managed with the earnings I got. Within approximately six months, I got tired and bored of being a babysitter and decided to look for an office position.

I checked with an employment agency, and they sent me on an interview with the New York Produce Exchange. They had an opening for a secretarial Girl Friday position. I went to the interview and was hired.

I worked for the secretary of the exchange as his secretary. I did well, and enjoyed my new work place. I was answering and routing phone calls, and I did some typing work as well. I was there at the exchange when the news came that President John F. Kennedy was assassinated.

About six months down the road, they were minimizing staff, and since I was the last one hired, I was also the first one fired. However, they liked my work ethics, and recommended me for a position at Meryl Lynch Pierce Fenner & Smith. Because of their recommendation, I was hired.

The office was on Madison Avenue. My position was as a cashier, documenting the stocks. Everything was handled by hand. That position required that I be bonded. On my employment application, I gave false information regarding my schooling. I entered a name of a high school in Israel, which I never attended.

No one had ever checked the accuracy of the information I gave until now. It took however about three months until they got a reply from the school in Israel, saying that my name was not on their records. In the meantime, I was doing a very good job for three months, which was lucky for me.

When personnel received the reply from Israel, I was called in to the personnel manager and confronted with that fact. I took a deep breath, and with tears in my eyes, told her the truth about my childhood, and lack of formal schooling. She accepted my truth and understood why I had to lie. Had I told the truth on my application, I wouldn't have been hired. I stayed at that job, and they even offered me an opportunity to become a stockbroker with their company, but I declined.

Chapter Two

Meeting My Husband

Changing Jobs Again

I left Meryl Lynch Pierce Fenner & Smith for a better and more interesting position. I was offered a job working for Zim Lines, the Israeli Steam Ship Company. I knew the general manager for Zim Lines in the U.S. from the times I worked at Lod airport as a ground hostess. He was than the airline station manager for TWA, and his name was Zeev Kis.

He told me that they had an opening for a reservation agent at their Fifth Avenue office and asked if I was interested in it. I didn't have to think twice for a response; this position was just down my alley. They had the S.S. Shalom, which was built with German compensation money received from Germany. (Germany was compensating Israel for the German/Hitler atrocities against Jews.) This was a beautiful and luxurious cruise ship, and the Zim office was selling reservations for the scheduled cruises.

The office was at 580 Fifth Avenue. We had a front office window on Fifth Avenue. There were three desks for the three of us who did cruise bookings. In addition to cruise reservations, I handled airline reservations and ticketing for company executives. I also worked at the pier prior to cruise departures, assisting in handling VIP passengers. This job was just right for me. I liked working with the public and being of service.

Going back to 1964 (Age 30)

In the winter of 1964, during winter break from the Hebrew Teachers School, I took a trip on a ski weekend for singles to upstate New York. On the way back from this trip, I met George Bell, who later became my husband. George sat beside me on the bus returning from the trip, and we chatted. All the women on the bus were after him to take them home. Once we'd arrive in New York, he had a car there and they knew it. I was the only one not harassing him to take me home. He liked that. George asked for my phone number, called me the next day, and we started dating.

He was a fun guy and introduced me to his friends who all lived in Far Rockaway, NY. George was thre years younger than I and so were his friends. They were intimidated by my worldliness and sophistication; however, George was fascinated and intrigued by it.

I found out that George loved kids; I saw how he played with one of his friend's children. That aspect touched my heart. I loved children too, and at age 30, I felt my biological clock ticking. Loving and wanting children was the main common denominator in our relationship. George did love me, though. He introduced me to his parents and his mother grilled me. I got a passing mark from her, and she approved.

About nine months into our courtship, George presented me with a diamond ring, and asked me to marry him. I said yes, and we got engaged. A wedding date was set for May 9, 1965. It was Mother's Day, quite an appropriate date for us.

George lived at home with his parents in a large house on Beach 9 Street in Far Rockaway until we got married. Our wedding took place at their home. It was a lovely wedding. My mother came from Israel for the wedding and my cousins from Long Island, New York attended as well as many friends and family members.

For our honeymoon, we went on a Caribbean cruise on the S.S. Shalom. We enjoyed the cruise. George was seasick while the ship was at sea, but we enjoyed the Caribbean ports of call. Our son, Robert Scott Bell, was conceived on the cruise. All in all, it was a delightful cruise and an enjoyable honeymoon.

Robert Scott Bell Was Born

On the second month of pregnancy, I scheduled an appointment with the OB/GYN. He predicted my due date to be February 23rd, and on February 23rd, 1966, our son Robert Scott Bell (Scottie) was born.

I worked at the Zim Lines until the middle of the seventh month of pregnancy. I would take the subway daily from Elmhurst Queens, where we lived in a rented apartment, to Manhattan.

We had two Siamese cats names PePe and Pancho. As a baby, Scottie would sleep with a pacifier in his mouth. One of the cats would often jump to his crib at night and pull the pacifier out of his mouth. It was a rubber pacifier, and the cats loved to chew on it. He would start screaming when the pacifier was taken out of his mouth, and I had to replace the pacifier to keep him quiet. The drug store where I bought the pacifiers was wondering what I did with so many pacifiers. I had to tell them that my cats loved them, too. The cats would sometimes sleep in his crib at his feet. They liked being next to him.

Our Marriage History and Being a Mother

I was 32 when our son was born. I was so ready for motherhood. In the morning of Feb 23rd, I went into labor, George drove me to New York University Hospital where Scottie was born. While I was being prepped for labor, George left the hospital. He was restless as usual and had to keep moving. After Scottie was delivered, the nurse was trying to find George, and apparently he went to work. The nurse told him that he had a son. Of course, he rushed to the hospital to see his new baby and congratulate me. After he saw Scottie, I asked him what he thought of our baby, as to me he was a gorgeous baby, and George said to me, "He's no Gregory Peck." I was not happy with that answer, but it is what it is.

I was ecstatic with my new baby. My in-laws were on a trip out of town when Scottie was born, and the only family that came to visit was George's Aunt Millie, who I adored. After about two days in the hospital, we brought Scottie home. I enjoyed so much taking care of my baby. I did not breast feed, as the doctor said that bottle milk was just as good as breast milk. He seemed to be allergic to every formula we gave him and would projectile vomit after every feeding. In spite of his vomiting, he gained weight and was quite a chubby baby. Thankfully, his vomiting stopped just before his first birthday. The pediatrician wanted to perform surgery on him if it didn't stop. It's as if he knew what would happen and just stopped vomiting.

Throughout his young life he was allergic to just about everything. It manifested itself in different ailments. When we moved to Florida we consulted an allergist who was a family friend, the allergy testing that was done on him showed that he was allergic to just about everything. The doctor started him on allergy shots, which he would get weekly, five shots in every arm. After a while, he received the shots monthly. I sometimes thought that when he drank water it would come out through his arms. Not really funny. For years, he got five shots in each arm.

In his 20s he decided to stop with the allergy shots on his own. A short while thereafter, he discovered true healing modalities with homeopathy, and he took on a healthy and holistic approach to his health, and his health began to improve.

Scottie was a gorgeous baby and very smart, too. Whenever I would call my mother-in-law to brag about something Scottie did, she would tell me, "Miki, have some humility." I thought to myself, why should I, I was just telling the truth.

It was very difficult to get Scottie to smile in the first year of his life, I now understand that he must have been quite uncomfortable, but could not yet speak to tell us how he felt.

Scottie never crawled like most babies do. At six months he would walk around his crib. And at seven months he walked around the apartment holding on to the wall or the furniture. By eight months, he took off walking on his own and a short while thereafter, running. He was always on the go, and I was right behind him.

I was told that if a baby does not go through the crawling phase, he is missing something in his development. I did not find this to be the case. George was a proud father, and loved being married to me.

George was addicted to sleeping pills and Valium when I met him. He had been in therapy for many years prior to meeting me. I met his therapist before we got married. He was a very kind man who cared much for George and his future. His name was Dr. Chlenoff.

George's mother, Dorothy, was a very domineering woman, very insecure within herself, and turned her insecurity to a domineering and controlling person. His father, William, was an optometrist by profession and an inventor; a very kind and intelligent man. However, in order to keep the peace at home, he acted like a doormat to his wife, and spent most of his time in the basement working on his inventions.

William, or Bill as he was called, was not very involved in the upbringing of his children. George had an older sister, Phyllis, and a younger brother, Robert. George was the middle child. He turned his energies outward and always had to be the joker in the crowd and the center of attention. Robert, George's younger brother, was the opposite; he was an intorvert and shy and was jealous of his brothers' outgoing personality. He loved George, though.

Robert made it through medical school and became a doctor in the field of radiology. George on the other hand, wished he could be more like his brother who became a doctor. George felt he was a disappointment to his parents who wanted him also to become a doctor. George would do anything for attention, he was very outgoing and always the life of the party. He covered up his inner insecure child very well.

I came into the marriage with a conviction that I could fix him. I saw the good in him, and knew I could help him reach his potential to become a more secure person. I had good intentions, but little understanding that we can't fix anybody but ourselves. It took me many years to learn this important piece of wisdom, but it didn't happen while we were married.

I did manage to help him reduce the frequency of using Valium and sleeping pills, and eventually he was able to sleep without taking sleeping pills. He continued seeing Dr. Chlenoff until we moved to Florida. I would sometimes go along to help better understand George and his issues.

George worked for his parents' company, Bell Craig, manufacturing barium. They later sold their company to C.B. Fleet Pharmaceuticals. The famous Fleet enema was one of their main products. C.B. Fleet hired George to train their sales staff on the new product they acquired from Bell Craig Company, and George became the sales and training manager for them.

In his new position, he felt powerful, and was very good at it; however, he did not know how to balance his work with his family life and obligations. When he would come home from work, he would be on the phone for hours with one of his sales representatives. Their conversation was more in the line of gossip, rather than productive business issues. I would ask him to please get off the phone and be present, help me with dinner, or play with Scottie, but he was in his own world.

He was not a partner in the marriage to me. I felt very alone, and put all my energies into mothering. It felt as if I had two children rather than a child and a husband as my partner.

In November 1966, when Scottie was nine months old, I received a phone call from my mother in Israel, and in the conversation she said, "By the way, your father died a week ago." I was shocked and upset in the manner in which I found out about his passing. I didn't have a chance to mourn his death and was upset at my mother for telling me as if she was talking about the weather. How insensitive of her. I later found out that he died of a heart attack.

By February 1967, we moved from our one-bedroom apartment in Elmhurst, Queens, to a two-bedroom apartment in Whitestone, Queens. Our new apartment was spacious with lots of windows in the living room overlooking the Whitestone Bridge and the L.I. sound. We decorated Scottie's bedroom with a nice child design linoleum floor, and our bedroom had a sliding door to the balcony. The kitchen was adequate, although it had no window, and I always liked to have a lot of light and sunshine. We lived on the third floor, the building had five floors. We made friends with a couple next door to ours, they had no children, but were very nice and fun neighbors to have.

The neighborhood had a lovely playground, a swimming pool, and tennis courts. We were moving up, and I liked our new place. I made new friends with mothers at the playground, and became involved with Women's American ORT organization. ORT stands for rehabilitation through training; the organization has schools throughout the world, and teaches vocation. Its moto is: Teach a man/women to fish and they will not go hungry. Their vocational schools taught self reliance. For one of the meetings, I was charged with producing a musical play that was to the tune of Fiddler on The Roof, with a story line relevant to ORT's philosophy. I enjoyed producing that play and it was a success.

We discussed having another child and planned the age difference to be at about 2½ years. I became pregnant and it was an easy pregnancy, although I needed my afternoon naps, which I took when Scottie would take his nap.

June 4, 1968 - Our Daughter Julia Was Born

When Scottie was 2½, our daughter Julia was born. I was scheduled for an induced labor, because I needed to make arrangements as to who would watch Scottie while I was away giving birth. In hindsight, I wish I had waited for nature to decide when I'd give birth, rather than schedule it to be induced by medicine.

The caudal injection I received to start the labor sent my body into an uncontrollable shaking. And in a very short while I had to call the nurse, as I felt the head coming out. They thought it would take longer for the injection to work. I was rushed to the delivery room, and Julia popped right out. This must have been a traumatic entrance for her into this world. I often wonder if that was not the cause of her emotional and neurological issues.

While I was pregnant with Julia, two of my friends who lived in our complex were also pregnant, the three of us had boys, and all wanted to have a girl, I was the only one who wanted another boy, because Scottie was such an easy baby, except for his allergies. My girlfriends gave birth to a second boy, and I gave birth to a girl. I was very happy and proud to have a girl and enjoyed having pink clothes for my little girl. When I would tell that story later in life, Julia apparently interpreted it as if I did not want her, which was furthest from the truth. But perception is reality, and so Julia's relationship with me when she was young was not a close one as I would have liked it to be. She was much closer to her father than to me.

As a young child, Julia exhibited extreme fear of separation. If we went to a department store, and if for a second she turned away from me, she would howl as if she had been lost and abandoned, while Scottie was happy running all over the place without a care or fear in the world.

I enjoyed living in Whitestone. I made friends with other mothers with young children like mine, and we would meet in the playground while the kids were playing. The first summer we spent there, we enjoyed using the swimming pool. Most of the mothers would play Mahjong, a tile game. Their kids were more placid than mine, but Scottie was always on the run, and I ran behind him. He was extremely independent as a child and would not sit still for a moment.

Time to Move Again

By 1970, our area began to suffer from crime. It became dangerous to use the elevator, as we did not know who would come in and rob us or kidnap our children. I began to feel restless and felt we needed to move. I always embraced change and trusted my gut feeling in handling change. George, on the other hand, was afraid of change and preferred the status quo. I began to nudge George that we needed to move to a safer place for the sake of the children.

One of my girlfriends, Ellen, had moved to Florida several months earlier and she told me about a new subdivision being built in Margate, Florida. George's job though, was in New York. I told him that as a good salesman, he could find a good job in Florida. To appease me, he began checking on jobs in Florida. I told him that no one will hire someone who lives in another state, and you have to commit to the move for something to happen. It was a Catch-22.

We Bought Our First Home in Florida

We took a vacation trip to Florida, visited Margate and the new subdivision, and while there we put a down payment on a house to be built on a canal, which would be ready for us within three months.

George's parents had already moved to Florida. We went to visit them and told them we put a down payment on a house. They said; "Are you crazy? Without a job here, you are buying a house?"

"Yes." I said, "It was all my doing."

I believe that we have to trust even before all the pieces are in place, and with that trust, the right outcome happens. Call me crazy, but this is the way I believe and the way I live my life—with trust.

We returned home, and I found out that George was afraid to move without having a job. He had agreed to put a down payment just to appease me, but in his mind he was going to cancel this purchase. This is understandable in hindsight; I was too strong-headed for him to oppose.

As luck or faith would have it, when we returned to New York we found out that an opening had become available in Florida for a sales manager covering the southeastern region. George asked the company for a transfer and they agreed. Everything fell into place; they even paid for the move.

I followed my gut feeling with complete trust that all would be fine, and it proved to be so. If we hadn't moved, and bought our first house, which at the time cost us $27,000, we would not have been able to realize the American Dream of home ownership later on.

Living in Margate was good. The kids enjoyed the Florida weather, we had a swimming pool, and George enjoyed running around the neighborhood flirting with the ladies and taking our marriage, and me, for granted. George was happy go lucky in his own world, and clueless as to my needs or feelings. I so much wanted to have a loving home and family to fill, which I missed as a child. But it seemed that I married a child who needed me more as a mother than as a wife. I did not share with him how I felt and kept my hurt feelings inside.

Maybe things would have turned out differently had I shared them with him, but I was too independent and self-reliant and put on a face as if all was okay.

Photos

Wedding Picture of my parents. Date July 27th, 1927

Miki, $1^{1/2}$ years old

Miki with Father and his friends

Miki with Mother at age $11^{1/2}$

Miki with sister Ruthie

Miki in police uniform, age 18

Miki with Mother and dog ChiCha

1956, Sinai Campaign, Ben Gurion deplaining with Miki and Renana
(Renana, Ben Gurion's daughter)

Miki, climbing on Jeep at Sinai Desert with Ben Gurion, Head of State

Walking the Sinai Desert, Chief of Staff Moshe Dayan, Ben Gurion, and Miki

Viewing Sharm El Sheik from tower

5 Bachelors and Miki in Mexico City

Israeli Art Center in Luasanne, Switzerland

Miki in bikini with cousin Harold Sack
in Long Island private beach club

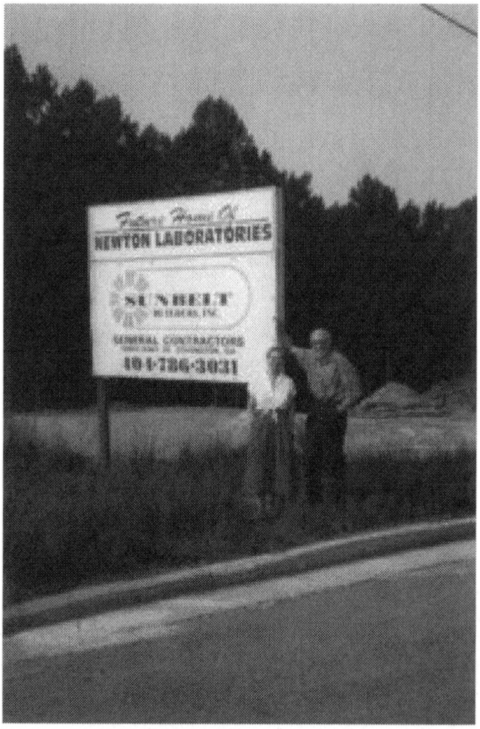

Miki and husband (Homeopath) Luc Chaltin
and new ground breaking for Newton Labs

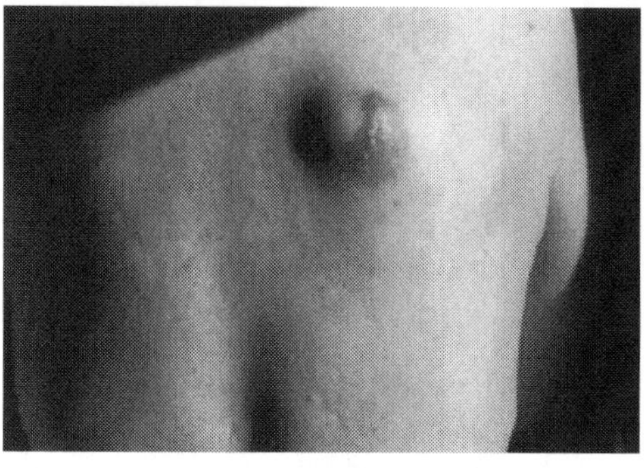

Miki's boil on my back

Chapter Three

Life in Georgia 1975

Three years after we moved to Margate Florida, George was transferred to Atlanta, Georgia. We took a trip to Atlanta to look for a house, and found the right house in the city of Stone Mountain. We made an offer and it was accepted, at the same time we managed to sell our house in Margate for $79.000. The house we purchased was a lovely contemporary style in the Cedar Park subdivision. It was on a cul-de-sac surrounded by lots of trees, and it had a large rustic cedar deck surrounding a swimming pool. Although we did not want the swimming pool, we accepted it and knew that we could close the deck over the pool and have a lovely deck nestled among the hardwood trees.

The neighborhood had a swim and tennis club, and the kids swam competitively against other community clubs. They went to Hambrick Elementary and later to Stone Mountain High. It was a very nice community. I became involved with the PTA and the kid's school activities.

We made friends in the neighborhood, and the kids made friends as well. The swim and tennis club made it easy to get to know our neighbors and it was conducive to making friends. It seemed like we were living the American Dream.

George loved Neil Diamond, and we started a Neil Diamond Fan Club. We had one meeting of the fan club members at our home. We often played Neil Diamond music, and whenever there was a live Neil Diamond Concert, George would queue all night to get good tickets to the concert for all of us.

We even traveled once out of state, I think it was to Birmingham, Alabama, to attend a Neil Diamond concert. We got there early, and George knew one of the stage guards who let us go behind the stage where we bumped into Neil Diamond. We struck up a conversation with Neil, and during the concert he acknowledged us by saying, "Hello to the Bell family from Atlanta." This was a thrill.

We lived above our means, however, and money and paying bills became an issue. We were always short of money before the end of the month. I wanted to get a job, but realized that I needed to get a high school degree first.

I Got My High School Diploma

I went to DeKalb Community College and explained my background to the school's admissions person. She suggested that my life's experience would help me, so I scheduled a date to take the high school equivalency test or GED as it is called. I did study to prepare for the test, and as I sat in the classroom taking the test, my hand and body began to shake, I could not control it. I felt fear, it reminded me of my childhood school time. The subject that terrified me most was math. I took a deep breath, and proceeded to answer the questions on the test as best I could. When it came to the math portion of the test, I decided to just guess. There was no way I could arrive at the right answer by calculating it. I finished the test within the allotted time, and hoped I passed.

I was thrilled to get my diploma in the mail on December 5, 1975. I passed—what a relief. In January 1976, I enrolled in college and took the classes, Principles of Psychology, Advertising and Sales Principles, and Music Appreciation. In advertising, we were given a project to invent a product. I invented a hand vacuum before there was such a product on the market. I enjoyed being a student, and did well.

I stayed in the school for two quarters, spring and winter of 1976. My grades were two As and one B. I loved and enjoyed being a student; however, I needed the GED in order to get a job to help supplement our household income. We were always behind and short of funds by the end of each month, we were living beyond our means, so reluctantly I dropped out of school and began looking for a job.

1977 - Becoming a Real Estate Agent

The real estate agent that sold us our house in Cedar Park became a family friend. Her name was Virginia Albey. Virginia was a very successful agent and she encouraged me to take their Real Estate course and become an agent.

I enrolled in the Real Estate Agents course given by Clover Realty. I do not remember how long the course took; it might have been three weeks or so. I took the final exam and in a letter dated April 25, 1977, from The Georgia Real Estate Commission, I was informed that I had successfully passed. I received my diploma as a Residential Specialist dated May 26, 1977.

With energy and determination, I jumped into the role of real estate agent. The first listing I secured was the home of the Azpell family. They lived on our street on Cedar Park

Drive. They were contemplating a move to Birmingham and had their home listed with another agent prior to my becoming an agent. They had no success in selling their home, so I was able to secure their listing. Within three weeks of my work on their behalf, their house was sold. That was less than one month after becoming an agent.

I kept a record of homes I sold in 1977, I sold ten homes, all between June and December 1977. The work of an agent was very consuming. Between previews of home for potential buyers coming to town, and servicing homes listed with me, I was very busy. Calls would come in at all hours of the day, night and weekends, but work never seemed to scare me. I liked the end result of seeing clients happy in the home of their dreams. In the first nine months of being an agent, I did nearly one million dollars in sales. The commission I earned helped our household expenses and paid for Scottie's Bar Mitzvah.

Our Marriage

George was travelling with his job, and I felt that being the excellent sales person that he was, he could earn a much better commission being a salesperson for items that would bring him a better income than selling Fleet Enema's and Summer's Eve Douche, which were the main products of C.B. Fleet Pharmaceuticals. But George could not entertain the thought of making a change. He was afraid of his own shadow and the thought of a change was too frightening for him.

I did not take this aspect of his personality into consideration. I was operating from my experience, and from my background of survival and embracing change. I did not try to walk in his shoes. It took me many years to recognize how wrong I was to push him as I did. He would just retreat into his own shell.

In June 1978, I talked him into taking a Career Management Evaluation course. I felt that with the proper guidance, he could overcome his fears and move on to a better position with a better income. He did as I wanted, but that did not help him in overcoming his fear of change. It just made money for the Career Management Company.

With regard to our children, here again, unfortunately, George was not a partner. We could never have a cohesive front as to discipline. George would never side with me when it came to discipline. I was on my own and frustrated. I needed to have a unified front when it came to Julia especially, she was more of an unruly child, and I needed a partner in a husband. Scottie was easy and self-motivated, a good student and a responsible child.

Julia on the other hand was not. It was impossible to get her up in the morning. She acted in a disrespectful manner to me or any authority; she helped herself to items of Scottie's clothing or my cosmetics, without regard or permission, and never put things back in their place.

George would always side with her. It seemed that they were working against me. She missed many school days because she would not get up. She also befriended a girl in the neighborhood I did not approve of, due to poor language and disrespectful behavior, but she did what she wanted, and George was always on her side. I just gave up on disciplining her, it was a no-win situation.

I was very busy in my work as a real estate agent, and it occupied much of my time. Maybe I wasn't a very good and attentive mother to Julia, who needed much more attention than Scottie. I did the best I knew, but it probably wasn't good enough.

1978-1979 - Saving and Preparing for Scott's Bar Mitzvah

We became members of a synagogue in order for Scott to prepare for his Bar Mitzvah. We belonged to Congregation Shearith Israel, and Scottie would go weekly to study his Haftarah portion in Hebrew. In the Jewish tradition, a boy at 13 is considered a man, and he has to study for about a year with the Rabbi or the Cantor to prepare for the reading of the Torah portion in Hebrew on his Bar Mitzvah. It is considered quite an honor for the boy to read from the Torah in front of the whole congregation and the invited guests on the day of his Bar Mitzvah in the synagogue.

I helped with teaching Hebrew at their Hebrew Sunday School, and Julia also went to the Hebrew School at the synagogue. The dues for membership were quite steep for us, and after the Bar Mitzvah, we didn't rejoin. With the commission I earned as a real estate agent, we were able to have a very nice celebration for his Bar Mitzvah.

Our house had a lovely wooded backyard with an above-ground swimming pool and a cedar wood deck built around the pool, making it look like an in-ground pool. We hired someone to close the deck over the pool since we really didn't want the pool.

We decided to use the backyard deck for the Bar Mitzvah. I hired a caterer and selected the menu. My mother came from Israel for the occasion, and the Bell family with aunts, uncles, great aunts, and cousins, also attended. The caterer provided round tables with festive white table cloths and the dishes as well. The caterer was Jewish and was known for their excellent selections of Jewish-style food. The guests were invited to come to our home after the service and we served a lunch menu buffet style. After the meal, the kids retired to play games in the front yard, our cousins also participated. The adults stayed to visit with one another, it was quite a warm day, and we later left the deck and went into our air-conditioned house to cool off and have dessert. It was a wonderful occasion for the family to get together. The Bar Mitzvah was held on May 12, 1979.

When it came time for Julia to study and prepare for her Bat Mitzvah, she declined the honor.

Chapter Four

Introduction to Convention Work

1978

By 1978, when Jimmy Carter was president, interest rates kept climbing from 6.75% in 1976, to 11% in 1978, and to 20.5% through 1981. This increase dried up the real estate market. No one could afford to take on a mortgage for 30 years at this high interest rate.

I was looking for other opportunities to supplement our income. In talking to a neighbor friend, I was introduced by her to part-time convention work. She said it was a fun way to make extra money. She gave me the number to call, and I made an appointment and was hired for the next convention that came to town. We worked as registration personnel.

I liked working conventions, and got to know and understand the business. What I did not like was the lack of professionalism. The women were more interested in chatting with each other than attending to the convention participants. They thought they were there to be entertained rather than delivering the service for which they were hired.

By 1980, I felt confident that I could provide this service to conventions in a much more professional manner. I had an idea and a vision that I would hire flight attendants on their off time to work the conventions. They are usually intelligent, attractive, and professional, and good at working with the public. I would institute a dress code of a navy or black skirt with a white blouse. I would add a Southern touch by having the girls wear a silk pink dogwood flower on their lapel. I was ready to compete against the company I was working for, but with a more professional approach.

While staying focused on creating a business that would secure a financial future for my children, I was contemplating to divorce George. I tried everything I could to push him, but he dug his heels in where he was, and was unable to move forward. It was quite frustrating for me, but I decided that I had to do all I could to secure a financial future. I knew that had I stayed married to George, we would end up depending on government assistance with no money or security in our old age. We had no savings, and we continued living above our means. This was not what I wished to see down the road for us.

1980 - A New Beginning in Business

I had the complete vision of what my new idea for business was going to be. What I was lacking, though, was the confidence that I could do it on my own. I felt I needed a partner to launch my business. I shared my idea with Maureen, a friend in our neighborhood. Maureen mentioned she had a good friend, a former stewardess for Eastern, who was looking for something to do. Maureen arranged for her friend Suzie to meet with me. I explained my business plan to Suzie at our first meeting, and I remember her saying to me, "You seem to know everything about how you see that business and what it needs, so why do you need me?" I am not sure I remember what my answer was, but we agreed to become partners. I was to be president and she would be vice president. I had a name for the business, Convention Administration and Sales Personnel, and we'd go by the initials CASP. A friend of Suzie's designed our logo and we were ready to incorporate.

Suzie later introduced me to her friend Jo Ann, who was also a former Eastern flight attendant. Jo Ann was interested in becoming a partner as well and Suzie suggested she become our sales manager. I agreed. It took several months to put the whole business plan together, and in May 1981, we were incorporated. I owned 38% shares, Suzie 37%, and Jo Ann 25%.

Both Suzie and Jo Ann were happily married, and the business for them was more of a fun activity. For me it was a matter of survival. I had just separated from my husband and filing for a divorce, and I needed the business income for survival. They were also both Southern girls, and I was from a world foreign to them. They did not understand my forward approach and honest personality.

For a year and a half we made our presence known in the convention industry. We became members of the Atlanta Convention & Visitors Bureau, Meeting Planners International, and Convention Management Association. Suzie and Jo Anne's husbands were connected to the media and we got some good publicity in the press as we began our new business enterprise.

We competed for accounts with the local convention personnel companies and the Atlanta Convention & Visitors Bureau. The hourly fee we charged was often the determining factor in securing a particular account. We became a force to be reckoned with.

The flight attendants we hired appreciated the opportunity to work conventions on their off time.

They worked as independent contractors, and signed independent contractor agreements.

It seemed that in time, Suzie and Jo Ann began to feel they no longer needed me. When I lost one account, The World of Concrete. Daniel Sladeck was the convention vice president and was a very tough negotiator. He did not like the fee I quoted and hired another company. They used this as an excuse to cause a separation.

The irony is that when I had my own business, without Suzie and Jo Ann, I managed to get the World of Concrete account. Mr. Sladeck was very pleased with the service my company provided, and in a letter to me dated March 16, 1984 he wrote:

> *Thanks for your excellent service and professional personnel you provided during the World of Concrete '84 in Washington D.C. I received many excellent comments on how courteous and helpful the registration personnel were this year. This is a credit to your ability to screen good personnel.*
>
> *My sincere appreciation for all your help and supervision.*
>
> *Best wishes to you in your future endeavors.*
>
> *Sincerely,*
> *Daniel J. Sladeck*
> *Vice President – World of Concrete Inc.*

After losing the account, Suzie and Jo Ann came to me and dictated what I could and couldn't do. They said I was a failure, and they couldn't follow a person who failed. They were obviously unaware of the fact that every successful person has endured some failures. Isn't that how we learn and grow to become better?

They ordered me to stay home, do the paper work, and refrain from interacting with the accounts. I was in shock. Between the two of them, they owned the majority of shares, and as long as they were in agreement with each other, I was out of luck and stuck.

I tolerated this situation for a very short time. I scheduled a meeting with them and suggested that it seemed that three is a crowd, and Jo Ann was undermining my value. I offered Suzie to side with me, or I would resign and become their biggest competitor. Suzie rejected my offer. I scheduled a meeting with our attorneys, Robert Goldberg and Mark Levick. At that meeting I gave my resignation, and we parted company.

I was very upset, and felt totally betrayed by two ladies whom I brought into a business that I envisioned and created. Leaving the attorney's office with tears in my eyes, I met with a girlfriend and related to her what had transpired; I was really upset. She stopped me cold and asked, "What is the name of your new company?" She was a godsend at this low moment in time, and I answered, "Miki Bell Enterpries."

Suzie and Jo Ann lasted in business less than six months, and then faded from the convention scene. My business on the other hand was thriving, and for 5½ years I worked very hard, about ten hours a day, seven days a week. People in the industry thought I had a large staff helping me, but I did it all by myself. It was not easy, but, you do what you have to do to survive, and I did just that. My company provided an excellent service unsurpassed by any other company and I was proud of that. I sometimes hired my son and my daughter to work conventions as well.

It's hard to see the benefits of an adverse situation when you are in the midst of it. In looking back, I realize they did me a favor. It allowed me to thrive in business on my own.

1982 - Contemplating Separation and Divorce

Our marriage had not been working for some time. I was thinking down the road what would happen if I stayed married to George. What I saw was not at all what I thought I deserved in a marriage. George was not a partner or a good provider. However, he was a loving father. I could envision that if I remain married, we would end up poor with nothing to fall back on as security.

We had no savings and George's job was not secure; in fact, C.B. Fleet kept reducing the commission percentages he would get from sales. The future with him looked bleak. We had no savings and no plans for retirement. I had to take action and rely on myself.

I told George I wanted to divorce him. He took it very hard, as I was the backbone of the marriage. Although I felt sorry for him, I had to think of my future and the future of our children.

In July 1982, I filed for divorce and he moved out. After much bickering back and forth, the divorce became final in April 1983. Part of the divorce agreement stipulated that when Julia became 18, I was to sell our house and we would split the proceeds.

George had a nervous breakdown after the divorce became final. He was hospitalized for some time. This helped him face some of his own issues; nevertheless, he kept resenting me for divorcing him. Late in February 1984, when Julia was hospitalized with bulimia and anorexia, I wanted her to be transferred to an eating disorder program rather than where she was, which was with teenagers with criminal backgrounds. He fought me, just to oppose me. He was unable to get over his pain and do what was best for Julia at the time. I was viewed as the evil bad women.

After several years, George made his own friends and his own life, at that time, we were able to have a civil and friendly relationship, which was important since we did have two wonderful children together.

George was always included and was welcome to come to my house when the children were over for dinner and on Thanksgiving. I held no animosity towards him, and he liked to be included and felt welcome, which he was. I did not want to do to him what my mother did to me. He was their father and they loved him. It was important for the children to keep him involved in their lives.

Later on, when the children got married and had their own children, he was a loving grandfather to our grandchildren. He would come to their school weekly to have lunch with them, and they loved it and loved him very much.

When George had a quadruple heart by-pass, he moved in with my son and my daughter-in-law Nancy. He lived with them for several years until he felt strong enough to rent an apartment for himself and live on his own.

1982 - Miki Bell Enterprises Is Thriving

I needed funds to re-start the business on my own, I had to create and print brochures, letterheads, envelopes, and business cards. I also needed to become a member of the Atlanta Convention & Visitors Bureau and Meeting Planners International, in addition to incorporating and paying attorney's fees. I figured that I needed at least $5,000 to begin. Having no money; I decided to ask for a bank loan.

I dressed in a professional navy suit with a pink blouse and went to meet with the bank manager at NBG on Memorial Drive in Stone Mountain. I presented my business plan, and my background, the banker was impressed and approved me for an unsecured business loan of $5,000. I was ready now to fly on my own.

I started to make sales calls to conventions that were scheduled to come to Atlanta. The Georgia World Congress Center had a list of future conventions with all the information as to whom to contact. This was the prospecting tool I used. I would sit in my office, which was downstairs in the house, and I would make my sales calls from my home office in the morning dressed in my comfortable house dress, while the kids were at school.

When going downtown for appointments with prospective clients, I would dress very professionally and make my presentation as to why my company was better than any of the competing companies. I already had a good name in the industry, and I was very well received.

Miki Bell Enterprises Becomes a National Company

I began to secure very good accounts, mostly Fortune 500 companies. Their conventions were held once a year in different cities. Since they were so pleased with the quality of personnel I provided in Atlanta, they began to hire my services for their conventions in other cities. Some of the companies that hired my services in other cities were The Million Dollar Round Table, National Association of Music Merchants, Canon, Cahners Exposition Group, and more.

My brochure heading read as follows:

IF YOU'VE BEEN AT A TRADE SHOW WHERE THE REGISTRATION PERSONNEL WERE GREAT! - CHANCES ARE…

MIKI BELL WAS THERE!

My picture was in the front of the brochure.

While outwardly I presented myself as a very secure and successful businessperson, I was alone wearing many hats in running my business, and I was stressed handling the children at home and portraying the professional business woman to the outside world.

On a personal level, I was going through turmoil. George's nervous breakdown due to my divorcing him painted me as an evil and uncaring women. People did not know what I was going through in my marriage. He was viewed as this very nice and friendly man married to this uncaring women. I was hurting and inwardly developed extreme abdominal pains and got an ulcer. I existed on Pepto Bismol, Tums, and Alka Seltzer, to alleviate the pain. No one knew the turmoil residing within me. I covered my personal problems well.

Julia's Illness

At home, I discovered that enormous amounts of food were disappearing, especially bread, which led me to discover that Julia was anorexic and bulimic. Julia was hospitalized for her own good. She was in three different hospitals over a period of time. The period of visiting the hospital, and participating in sessions with other parents at the hospital chaired by the psychologist, was frustrating to say the least. Beside it being painful, there was a lot of blame going around, rather than finding a healing solution. It seemed a no-win situation. I felt so inadequate and unable to help. Julia harbored tremendous resentment towards me and viewed me as this evil mother who did not love her or care about her. It was hurtful. I was crying on the inside, but mostly wanting so much to help and could not.

Julia was later diagnosed with having the handicap of a mood disorder, ADHD and an enxiety disorder. She is very bright and insightful, caring and loving, but could not help herself in areas that were important in holding a job or being orderly and on time. She operated with her own internal clock, which had nothing to do with anybody else's.

On Scottie's 30th birthday in February 1996, Julia met her husband to be, David Guise. David was working at a health food store, and this is how Scottie met him and invited him to his party. David saw Julia, and was attracted to her; they began to date, and a short while later, got married.

Julia gave birth to two wonderful boys, Jeremy and Benjamin. The marriage ended in divorce when her youngest son, Benjamin was 15 months old. Julia was on her own to bring up the boys. She did the best she could under the circumstances in spite of the challenges she had. She is an over-protective mother and a very loving and caring one.

David, before their divorce was final, met a lady on the internet and began seeing her, a divorcee who lived in Florida with her three children. He married her and moved to Florida, a move he later regretted. He divorced her after about three years of marriage.

Jeremy was born on April 18, 1997 and Benjamin on April 12, 2000. Julia delivered Jeremy at my home with a midwife, and Ben was also delivered at home with a midwife.

Today, at the end of 2012, Jeremy is 15 and Ben is 12. They are wonderful boys, and Julia is a devoted mother to them. She is doing the best she can as a single mom with an emotional handicap. I am involved in their life and help as much as I can. Julia became a Jehovah's Witness and is very devoted to her belief. She loves doing service by knocking on peoples' doors, hoping to convert them, just as she was when someone knocked on her door. She says that doing service to her is like getting oxygen to breath. Well, I am glad she found her calling and it brings her joy. She loves reading the Bible and can recite it mostly by heart.When they were married, David wanted to have his own Health Food Store; I helped him get a bank loan to purchase the store, which was for sale at the time. I introduced David to my banker with whom I had good business relationship, and vouched for David. David provided a business plan as the banker requested, and the banker approved him for the loan based on my recommendation.

David liked owning the health food store, which was called, Better Way Natural Foods. He loved helping people with their issues and was very good at it. He was a hard worker; unfortunately David was impatient by nature and wanted a faster growth for his business. He introduced too much automation to expedite procedures, which resulted in too many bills his small store could not handle and the business could not afford. Several years later, he had to declared bankruptcy. I felt very bad for David and my banker who trusted my recommendation in giving David the business loan. However, the outcome was out of my hands.

Back to My Business

In addition to registration personnel, my company also provided interpreters, hostesses, and sales assistants. I created a complete meeting planner company. I wrote articles in trade publications with tips on how to get the most out of your convention experience. I created and hosted a seminar for exhibitors on the dos and don'ts of creating a successful exhibit. I received many letters of accolades from clients serviced by my company and created a presentation portfolio with the letters I received to show prospective clients.

When hired to service a convention in another state, I would put an ad in the local news paper. When people responded, I would schedule interviews to select the right people for specific positions. I was able to read people well and train them to be the best that they could be. The clients were very pleased, as the letters I received indicate.

I was always on-site, supervising to make sure all went smoothly and professionally.

The registration area is the first encounter an attendee has upon arriving at the convention or trade show. There are no rehearsals in conventions. It's up to the registration personnel to make the attendees feel welcome and not frustrated due to poor handling of their registration process. My people delivered the best and most professional service.

Eckankar - A Spiritual Path

In December 1984, I was making sales calls to future conventions coming to Atlanta in 1985; this needed to be made at least six to nine months prior to the convention date. One of the conventions scheduled to come to the GWCC (Georgia World Congress Center) was Eckankar; they were based in California. I had never heard the name Eckankar before and had no idea what they were about, so I called their number and told the lady who answered the phone about my company and the services provided. She told me that their convention works only with volunteers, and my services would not be needed. I thanked her for her time and asked her what Eckankar was and she told me it was a spiritual path teaching spiritual principals. I told her I'd be interested in receiving information about them. She said she would be glad to send me information.

That afternoon, when Scottie came back from his first year at Emory University, at age eighteen, he placed a book on my desk titled, *Eckankar, Key to Secret Worlds.* I was perplexed to say the least. I told Scottie I had just spoken to Eckankar a few hours earlier and asked them for information, and here he was with this book.

He told me he was visiting his friend, Alex, in our neighborhood, saw that book and that it looked interesting, and he borrowed it. (Talk about speedy information from Eckankar). I immediately began reading the book and so did Scottie. As we finished reading it, we both felt we needed to belong to this organization. It resonated with both of us. We looked them up in the phone book, and found out that there was a group locally that held Eckankar meetings. We called, got the time and place, and drove to the meeting.

We were hooked. It spoke to me at a time when I so needed to find inner peace and learn how to deal with the stress in my life. They had study groups called satsang, they taught meditation, and their study materials were so profound and helpful to Scottie and me. I liked the fact that they were a spiritual organization rather than a religion, since I did not care much for organized religion. It helped me find inner peace and taught me how to better deal with my stressful life situation.

They later became a religious organization in order to receive the tax benefits afforded religious organizations but not spiritual ones. This was okay with me. I remained a member of Eckankar for many years and Scottie and I made many great friends.

Miki Bell Firm Named Outstanding

The Georgia Small Business Council named me Outstanding Business Owner of the year in 1985. The article wrote: ..."with an initial unsecured loan of $5000 from NBG, Ms. Bell started her business, Miki Bell Enterprises Inc. in 1982. In 1984, she achieved a growth of 144%. Ms. Bell is a meeting planner and personnel and talent supplier to the trade show industry nationwide. Ms. Bell services conventions from coast to coast."

My Memberships in Organizations and Involvement

1982 - 1988 member Atlanta Convention & Visitors Bureau
1983 - 1988 member of Meeting Planners International
1985 - 1988 member Atlanta Business and Professional Women's Club
1986 -1987 Secretary/Treasurer for Southeastern National Assoc. of Exposition Managers
1986 - Elected Delegate to the White House Conference on Small Business
1987 - 1988, President of Atlanta Business and Professional Women's Club

So, my business became national, I had a knack of reading people well, and finding the right talent for each specific position needed. Because my personnel were far superior to other companies, I was hired to provide my services in other states, such as New York City, Boston, Washington D.C., Houston, Chicago, and San Francisco.

Unfair Competition between Government and Private Industry

I encountered unfair competition form the Atlanta Convention & Visitors Bureau, AC&VB, which is a government entity.

I was a business owner and a dues-paying member of the AC&VB. They had an unfair advantage over securing clients for conventions coming to Atlanta, and they competed with their own dues-paying members. The AC&VB is subsidized by its members as well as by government. By 1986, the people I introduced and trained in the industry, now became part of the general personnel pool that the AC&VB could hire from.

The AC&VB was in a position to offer clients free registration hours, which I was unable to do, plus other benefits. I, on the other hand, had to pay my personnel for every hour they worked, so I was not in a position to offer free personnel hours. My profit margin was very small on each personnel hour. My supervising time on site was not charged to the client, so basically I was breaking even and only just able to pay my bills.

By the latter part of 1986, my business was hurting. The AC&VB had the upper hand in securing the registration business. The product I was delivering to the industry was personnel, which is very different from a product that sits on the shelf waiting to be purchased.

My personnel were free to go wherever the work was. Since the AC&VB had secured the accounts with their unfair advantage over me, they were able to hire the professional personnel I had introduced and trained in the industry, and they were benefiting from my innovative approach.

I saw the handwriting on the wall. I couldn't fight City Hall, and so with few conventions to service, I generated very little income. I had no savings, and nothing to fall back on. I had no money to pay my mortgage, or anything else. I knew that with financing I could better compete with them, but it was a Catch-22.

I called my cousin Harold Sack in New York and asked him to loan me $5,000 to tide me over until I managed to find another source of income. Bless his heart, he immediately sent me $5,000 and I was able to pay my bills for that month.

I began looking for a job within the meeting planning industry, but the response I got was that I was overqualified for the job. I was an entrepreneur, and it did not fit corporate America.

Chapter Five

I Find a Buyer for Miki Bell Enterprises, Inc.

While searching for a job, a good friend whom I met while servicing The Million Dollar Round Table suggested I call on a friend of his, the owner of an insurance agency, to see if they would hire and train me to become an insurance agent.

I made an appointment, and went to meet them. At the meeting I showed my portfolio with all the letters with accolades from previous clients. They were very impressed and were ready to hire me. However, they then told me that they have a client who owned a personnel agency, who deals with unskilled labor, and they knew this client was interested in servicing the convention/ trade show industry. However, it is not easy to start servicing this industry without extensive experience. I had that experience, and was very well-known and respected in this industry. They thought my expertise in that arena would be of interest to their client, and I said I would be interested in meeting with them. While I was at their office, they called that client and described my business to them. They were interested, and we scheduled a meeting at their office for the next day.

At the meeting they looked at my portfolio, were very impressed, and asked if I would be interested in selling them my business and remaining as its Executive Director. I shared with them the difficulty I had encountered with the AC&VB being an unfair competitor, and that I had been losing business to them. I felt that with this new backing, I would have a better chance to compete.

They asked me how much I wanted for my business, and I asked for $150,000 after some negotiations we agreed on a selling price of $100,000 with the following stipulations:

$5,000 to be paid to me on 2/17/86

$25,000 to be paid to me upon closing, in about six weeks

$35,000 to be paid to me one year after closing

$35,000 to be paid to me two years after closing

An employment contract was prepared by their attorney to begin March 1, 1986. My position would be Executive Director with an annual salary of $35,000 + 20% net profits and a life insurance policy of $250,000 payable to the corporation. It felt good to finally have backing, an office, and have the financial support I needed to compete in this arena.

I immediately paid back the $5,000 loan to my cousin Harold Sack. I was so happy to be able to do that. I bought myself a red Toyota Celica convertible and turned in my Nissan as part of the payment. I splurged. I felt I deserved this lovely car.

I wrote press releases and letters to clients letting them know of my new affiliation. At their office, I was introduced to Susan who was going to learn the business as my assistant. (Susan later tried to undermine me, and take my position in the company.)

We created new brochures with the new name, Miki Bell & Associates, Convention & Management Services. We rented office space at the CNN Center.

From my office, I could see the news anchors doing their news reporting live. The new brochure reflected the changes to a computerized registration, which became the trend, instead of a typewriter for badges.

My background was featured in the new brochure as follows:

> For nearly a decade, Miki Bell has provided outstanding registration services to countless conventions and trade shows around the country. With representatives in several cities, Miki Bell & Associates is continuing to serve the growing needs of the industry with top quality, dependable service....
>
> Miki Bell, founder and Executive Director, is known for leadership, innovativeness and professional dedication. Miki has published several articles for business and community in trade publications and is currently serving as Secretary/Treasurer of the Southeastern National Association of Exposition Managers (NAEM) chapter. Miki is also the '87 - '88 President of the Atlanta Business & Professional Women's Club and sits on several boards in an advisory capacity and committee chair.
>
> Early in 1986, Convention Connection Inc. acquired Miki Bell Enterprises. This timely acquisition enabled necessary growth and the addition of some important

> services, such as Advanced Computerized Registration and Plastic Card Embossers. At Miki Bell & Associates, our absolute commitment to providing exceptional support to those organizing conventions remains unsurpassed. New technology is ever emerging, and we can be counted on to continue offering the most advanced convention management services available.

I continued making sales calls and doing my best to generate business. The competition with the AC&VB was still tough. I got some business, but lost some as well.

Chapter Six

Creating ISBPS

International Society for Business & Professional Singles, Inc.

In 1987, I got an idea for creating a Singles Organization. Business seemed to be going well, but I had no personal life besides work. I was interested in meeting someone special, but since I did not frequent bars, I had to create the venue to meet single men of quality.

Most singles organizations I saw advertised in the newspapers were either affiliated with a church or with some dysfunction, with a need for an outside source to make one happy.

My approach and idea was to create a singles organization catering to business professionals. I would provide lectures on topics relating to one's individual responsibility to be happy, not looking to an outside source to find happiness.

I presented my idea to my boss at Convention Connection and offered them a partnership in this new venture. They declined, but gave me permission to pursue the venture on my own. I did that on my own time from home.

In May 1987, I incorporated The International Society for Business and Professional Singles. Following the incorporation, I sent out press releases and scheduled the first meeting. The inaugural meeting took place in August 1987. I created a flyer featuring the purpose and benefits of ISBPS, as follows:

> **PURPOSE:** To bring a focus to the value residing within each individual. To network in a cross-cultural environment resulting in improved communications, expanded horizons and friendships.
>
> **BENEFITS:** Networking with a diverse group of people enhances business and personal contacts. Staying current with professions and industries outside one's own sphere is crucial in today's fast changing Information Age. ISBPS provides a quality environment for interaction via personal contacts. The programs provide an expanded overview into diverse business and personal arenas.
>
> **QUALITY:** ISBPS respects the VALUE of YOUR TIME by providing a quality environment with quality programs that foster sincere exchange of information. Unlike "strictly social" groups, where one is likely to encounter a superficial and guarded atmosphere, the educational focus of our programs allows people to feel comfortable and be themselves.
>
> **AGES:** The ages of members and guests range from 25–50+

MEETINGS: We meet twice a month on the 2nd and 4th Thursday.

Ramada Inn at I-85 & Shallowford Rd.

DUES: Annual membership dues are currently $55.00. Cost to participate in meetings: $5.50 for members and $11.00 for guests.

(Attendance of meetings is a justifiable business expense)

Some of the meeting topics were: "Are Men & Women Really That Different, Enhancing Your Career Through Team Play, The Globalization of Industries and Its Impact on Atlanta and You, Laughter and its healing Effects, The Mystery of Making Video Presentations, The Dynamics of Networking, Is your Career Giving You As Much As You Are Giving It?, When Your Body Talks, Do You Listen?, Uncover the secret Message of your Dreams, and much more.

A special fun and memorable outing and activity I remember was on a July 4th weekend in 1988. We drove to Greenville, South Carolina for the Freedom Weekend Aloft. We had our own hot air balloon pilot and the feeling of flying in a hot air balloon was exhilarating.

In November of 1987, I produced the first newsletter, featuring an article titled, "The Quality of the Individual," which is a topic dear to me.

For the newsletter, I solicited members to write their thoughts about being a member of ISBPS. I will quote one of the members' inputs: "Most singles join singles organizations to meet singles of the opposite sex with similar interests, lifestyles and career compatibility. Many singles groups offer this primary objective. But few, if any, offer other advantages that ISBPS offers. This is an emphasis on personal growth and individual development. ISBPS brings into focus the responsibility of the individual for his or her own growth and happiness. I have been in and through most phases of single life, and this organization offers the basic philosophy that I need and, in my opinion, most singles need: 'Individualism in concert with other individuals. Think about it!" By: J.K. Advertising Sales Executive.

Scottie was very helpful to me. He was named Secretary in the incorporation papers. He helped me with the computer in producing the flyers and newsletters. He always attended the meetings and was the official photographer. My former husband, George, often attended the meetings as well.

I met some great people, and the members appreciated the quality of the environment I created. It was not at all profitable though; I just broke even. The profit would have come with an increase in numbers of memberships.

It seemed that the masses were not too interested in our quality meetings. My meetings appealed to a small and precious number of people. The usual number of people attending a meeting was around 30, and we had a base of about 35 to 50 members.

Meeting My Second Husband - Luc Chaltin

In October 1989, I received an application for membership in the mail from a new prospective member, Luc Chaltin. He addressed his note with the application to Mr. Miki Bell, as he thought Miki was a man. He was surprised when he came to the meeting and saw that I wasn't a man.

Luc was from Belgium, and told me that he was a homeopath. I had no idea what a homeopath was and asked him to tell me about it. We were interrupted in our conversation, and I truly wanted to find out what it was, so I invited him to my home later that week to meet my girlfriend, Sultana and me.

He shared with us his background, what he was doing, and what homeopathy was all about. He said he had many patients he was treating, and that he travelled out of state every three months to see and follow up with his patients as well as see new patients.

I shared with him my business background, as well as my health issues. He seemed very interested and said he wanted to open a laboratory for homeopathy, but did not have the necessary business background. He had already incorporated the name for his future lab in 1987, called Newton Labs, Inc. This was his dream still to be accomplished. It seemed that my business background was a perfect fit for what he wanted to create.

My friend, Sultana, sensed that we were interested in each other and excused herself. We went to a movie that evening and began to date. A romance ensued.

Back to Miki Bell & Assoc. & Convention Connection

It seemed that Convention Connection had unrealistic expectations as to the revenue that could be generated in a short time. I worked hard and did my best to generate business, but what I generated did not meet their unrealistic expectations.

By September of 1987, I was told that the business projections they expected from me were not met, and I was given an ultimatum in the next 90 days to generate gross sales of $15,000 per month, and if by mid December 1987, I had not raised the gross sales to this minimum, my employment with Miki Bell & Associates would be terminated.

I responded in a letter explaining the nature of the convention business. A business needs to have long-range commitments and planning. Theirs was an expectation of an immediate return on their investment based on my contacts. This was unrealistic to say the least.

Clearly, they felt they had my name and contacts, so they no longer needed me. They had Susan ready to fill my shoes, and they still owed me the last installment of $35.000, which was due in March 1988.

I contacted an attorney, as it was a clear a breach of contract. I tried to sue them, and pursued communications with them through my attorney until May 1988. The attorney's fees became a burden and the cost of going to trial was too much for me to handle, so I just gave up and moved on.

May 1988 - Looking For a Job Again

I got a job in a personnel agency called A-One Service Personnel, as a recruiting agent for their corporate clients. I would interview prospective employees for specific clients' needs.

My activities with promoting ISBPS continued during this time. My life was busy. My son Scottie lived at home while attending Emory University. Julia was living in Savannah, and I was also on the board of our condominium association.

I had health issues, and besides my ulcer, I had lower back pain and couldn't sit longer than half hour before the pain would begin, I also had pain in my left foot around my big toe. I went to a podiatrist, who arranged an elevation for my shoe but also suggested I needed surgery, which I could not afford. I had no medical insurance, and I also had a small tumor growth on my back.

Chapter Seven

Flashback - Visits to Israel

When Scottie was 3½ and Julia was a year old, George, myself, and the children flew to Israel to visit my mother and friends. Upon arriving at the airport at passport control, they wanted to write Scottie's name in my Israeli passport, which would have made him an Israeli citizen for life.

Having been born in Israel, I have to enter the country on my Israeli passport, even though I am now an American citizen. According to Israeli law, once an Israeli, always an Israeli, and the children of Israeli citizens are considered Israelis as well, even though they were not born in Israel.

I did not want Scottie to become an Israeli citizen without his consent, and he was too young to make that decision. It would also have meant that when he turned 18, he would be required to serve in the Israeli army. So just before the immigration officer was about to add him to my Israeli passport, I said that Scottie is my husband's son from a previous marriage. I surprised myself with that quick thinking and a solution to the situation. My mother was very proud of me for instantly coming up with such a good story.

We had a lovely visit; the children enjoyed the beach, which was the highlight of our visit. Julia was too young to remember the trip. Scottie at 16 went back and spent a summer in Israel as a student studying science and microbiology at the Hebrew University in Jerusalem. He enjoyed it and excelled in science. Julia also spent a summer in Israel when she was 16. This was an enjoyable visit for her.

After divorcing my second husband, Luc, (more on this later), I would fly to Israel to visit my mother and my friends. I would usually go in the month of May, which is a great time to visit Israel. It is not too hot yet, and the sea is absolutely gorgeous. My sister Ruth would come from London at the same time, and we would both stay at our mothers' apartment.

Our mother did not approve of us visiting (our sister) Nava, and we had to lie to her when we would visit her. After several times of having to lie, we decided that she'd better accept the fact that Nava is our sister, and we have the right to visit her, whether she approved or not. We suggested that she come with us and see for herself how nice Nava and her family were. She finally agreed to come with us, and indeed she realized how nice Nava was and what a wonderful cook she was. She would prepare a table with lots of delicious dishes, and my mother enjoyed her food, and liked her family as well. What a relief it was for us to no longer have to lie.

We always enjoyed our visits in Israel. The people are so friendly and open. Israelis are very honest, and one knows who one's friends are. Their homes are always open and welcoming. They entertain their guests with lots of wonderful homemade cakes and Israeli dishes. Israeli's live in the present moment, since life there is always fraught with danger. They go out a lot to restaurants, the theater, the movies, art galleries, and to concerts. Israeli's are very sociable and cultured.

Ruthie and I enjoyed the beach and we would go every morning for several hours. We would swim and sunbathe. The Mediterranean Sea is beautiful; the sand is soft like powder and very clean. The Tel-Aviv municipality keeps the beaches clean by sweeping it every night, so when you come in the morning it is pristine. In the evening we loved to watch the sunset while sitting in a café on the beach. Watching the sunset is breathtakingly beautiful; the whole sky turns red and orange, as the sun slowly sets behind the horizon.

Every Saturday morning, around 10 a.m., about 100 people gather on the beach between Frishman and Gordon streets for Israeli folk dancing. The music and the dances are stunning to watch. People of all shape and ages dance for hours. It is a treat to watch and listen to this beautiful music, which touches one's heart. It is very special indeed, and I always look forward to it whenever I visit.

I always enjoyed reconnecting with my friends in Tel Aviv when I would visit. Ruthie did not have many friends since she left at age seventeen. I, however had quite a number of good friends, and when I would come, we would pick up just where we left off. Even though we did not communicate between visits, our friendships stayed intact and we were always happy to reconnect.

My mother lived by herself on the third floor of our apartment building. She was agile and active. She would go to the beach for a swim every morning around 5:00 a.m. She loved the sea. Afterwards, she would keep busy sweeping the yard and then wash the stairs. To reach the third floor, she would climb 45 stairs. Her physical activities must have contributed to her good health.

Mother Was Wating To Die But Not Alone
Dec. 1998

I would call my mother regularly, about once a week, to check on her since she was alone, and my calls helped to brighten her day. She was getting on in years, and towards her 90s she sounded depressed and told me that she was tired of living, and had nothing to live for anymore.

In December 1998, I decided to fly to Israel with my daughter, Julia, and grandson, Jeremy, hoping that seeing her granddaughter and great-grandson would cheer her up. Jeremy was one year old at the time. It was unusual for me to go to Israel in December, but she sounded so depressed that something in me urged me to visit her.

When we arrived, she did not seem too interested in anyone else but me. So we arranged for Julia and Jeremy to stay with Nava, and I stayed at home with her.

The first Saturday we were in Israel, Nava invited us to come for Shabbat dinner. Shlomo was scheduled to pick us up around 1:00 p.m.

That morning was December 19, 1998. While I was still asleep; my mother was up early doing her usual chores: cleaning the yard, watering the plants, and washing the stairs. By the time I woke up, she had breakfast ready. After I ate, she wanted me to cut her hair, which I did. She always liked the way I'd cut it. As she was sitting in her bedroom in front of a mirror, and I was cutting her hair she suddenly said, "I wish I could go to sleep and not wake up." So I told her, "Why don't you ask God?" And she said, "He doesn't listen to me."

After I finished cutting her hair, she took a bath and dressed up; we were standing in the kitchen. She asked me to tweeze her eyebrows, which I did. As I was tweezing her eyebrows, she suddenly said, "Oye, I have a sharp pain in my chest." With that, she ran to her bedroom and collapsed in an armchair. I ran behind her I put my hand on her forehead and held her hand, and her breath came out rapidly for a second or two, and then she was with God.

She held off dying until someone would be with her; she was afraid to die alone. When it happened, I was not sure if she died or just fainted. I was shaken and called Nava and told her what happened, and then called for an ambulance. Shlomo was already on his way to help out. The paramedics came and declared her dead. They took her down the stairs on a stretcher and to the morgue.

We called my sister Ruthie, and she immediately arranged a flight and was in Tel Aviv the next day. I went with Shlomo to their house, and I was numb the rest of the day. I was sad in a way, but also relieved that she did not die alone, and I was there with her when it happened.

Mother died on a Saturday, and the funeral took place on Sunday, the next day. In the Jewish religion, one needs to be buried within 24 hours of death.

I never attended a funeral and burial in Israel, and this was a shock. The body of the deceased is carried on a stretcher covered with a sheet. The mourners walk behind while a Rabbi prays on the way to the burial site. Upon arriving at the freshly-dug grave, the body is dumped in, and sand covers the deceased.

In the Bible it is said, "From earth you come and to earth you shall return." (paraphrased) No casket is used, so that the body will decompose and become one with the earth.

My friends, Bentz as well as a few other friends, and Nava and Shlomo attended the funeral, and Ruthie and I returned to my mother's apartment. It felt empty and strange.

On Friday evening, the night before my mother passed away, Bentz came over to help me assess mother's situation and to talk her into moving into an assisted living facility, since it was not good for her at the age of 92 to continue living alone. We discussed several options available to her, and also had a doctor's appointment for her for Monday morning. We had no idea that the next day she would be gone.

Ruthie and I were left to take care of whatever was needed. My flight to Atlanta with my daughter and grandson was scheduled less than a week later. There was much to be done in a short time.

On Tuesday morning, we got a call from a person who said he heard we had an apartment to sell, and he had a wealthy individual interested in buying it. His name was Tamir Yavetz. Although we were still in mourning, we agreed to have him come over to hear his proposal.

It seemed that Bentz told him about our mother passing and that since Ruthie and I lived overseas, we might be willing to sell. Tamir Yavetz came over and gave us a song and dance routine for a quick sale.

I was ready to move on, since it was difficult to handle the business aspect of selling the apartment from overseas, so we negotiated and agreed to sell. My sister however, was not ready to let go, and agreed reluctantly. Tamir said he had an attorney by the name of Doron Maron that would draw up the contract; we would get some money up front and the balance later on. We went like sheep to the slaughter to sign the contract and I flew back home a few days later.

When my sister returned to London, she realized how devastated she was that we sold the apartment, which was actually three apartments. She felt that we were taken advantage of and she was right. So she decided to fight. She related what had happened to her good friend and a wonderful attorney and author, Aubrey Rose. Aubrey gave her a name of a friend in Israel that could connect her to a good attorney in Tel-Aviv. She took the next flight to Israel and was ready to move mountains to reverse the sale.

As it was revealed later, we were scammed by crooks who did not intend to pay the balance owed on the sale, and we were involved in court with them for a couple of years. The sale was finally reversed, and we were again the owners of the apartments. The best part of this experience, if there is such a thing, is that we found the best attorney ever, Rami Puri. He saved the day and managed to cancel the contract, which was not an easy thing to do, and we got our property back.

The attorney, Doron Maron, who had us sign the selling documents, was disbarred, and he escaped Israel to another country, and then was later brought back and is serving jail time—not for what he did to us, but what he did to other clients.

Our attorney, Rami Puri, and his wife, Tami, became good friends of ours. Whenever we come to Israel, we are invited to their home for dinner, and sometimes, if time permits, we meet at a restaurant in Tel Aviv. They have three lovely boys, and it is a family that exudes love and harmony rarely seen. We love them as family, and they feel the same towards us; they are friends for life. If anyone ever needs a real-estate attorney in Israel, the very best attorney they can get is Rami Puri. We would trust him with our life.

Chapter Eight

My Sister's Devastating Accident

July 11, 1961 - Age 33

On one of my flights to London as a stewardess, I went to visit my sister. She was not at home, but I knew she went to get her daughters from school and should be home shortly. While waiting for her outside, a neighbor approached me and said that she saw my sister's car was involved in an accident and that my sister was taken by ambulance to the hospital. The girls were all right and their father, Nat, had collected them.

The girls had minor glass cuts, and were shaken from the experience, and I was not able to go to the hospital to see how my sister was, as I had a flight scheduled later that night.

As it turned out, a friend from Israel, Hadassah Klatchkin, was in London, and my sister had been driving her around shopping all day. By the time she went to pick up her daughters from school around 4:00 p.m., she was dehydrated and exhausted and fell asleep at the wheel.

She awoke up after hitting a parked car and her head hit the windshield, which her head shattered. She had severe cuts to her eye and face.

As she was wheeled to the emergency room, an eye specialist was on his way out of town for a conference. A taxi was waiting to pick up the eye specialist on his way to Scotland. As my sister was wheeled in, he was summoned to take care of her, since her eye socket was hanging by a thread. He sent the taxi away, put on his operating grubs, and proceeded to operate on her eye trying to save her sight, and than suture her cut up face. He did his best to save her eye, which he did, but her eyesight in that eye is almost zero.

She underwent extensive surgeries to repair the cuts to her face and lips. She was never the same after the accident. All her life up to this point, her identity was associated with her good looks. Now that her external beauty was gone, she felt very depressed and wanted to die, but she had two small children to take care of. The accident was a catalyst for my sister to find herself and her spiritual identity and a life of service to others. She lost her outer beauty and found her beauty within.

It took a couple of years for the wounds to heal. While slowly healing, she would take walks in the park across the street from her home. One day, while walking in the park, it began to rain. There was a library at the other end of the park, so she entered the library to wait for the rain to subside. While there, she began browsing the bookshelves and found her hand being guided towards a spiritual book. She had been looking for some time for answers and solutions to deal with her depression and her death wish. This book led her to the beginning of her spiritual journey. It took her many years to find inner peace and emotional security. It seemed that this accident was a wake-up call to become the wonderful spiritual person and healer she became.

Her husband, Nat, developed a very successful business. He built a factory manufacturing raw plastics. He was an excellent businessperson and made a lot of money. He was a shallow person, though, and spent money on expensive cars, expensive clothes, and anything to show off his success.

They built a Scandinavian-style house with a swimming pool. He imported marble and leather from Italy, and imported leather furnishers from Italy as well. He also bought an Ashton Martin, a Rolls Royce, and a Lamborghini, although not all at the same time.

Their daughter, Diana, liked to ride horses, so he bought her a horse with a trailer and hired a trainer. She was good at show jumping and attended many horse shows and did very well at it. Diana however, was not a happy child, in spite of, or maybe because, she got everything she wanted.

He provided Ruthie with a housekeeper/nanny to help with the children and housekeeping. They had another daughter called Danielle, whom they nicknamed Poppie.

Years later, when Diana was married and was pregnant with her first child, Ruthie found out that she too was pregnant. They both had boys. Diana's son was named Jeremy, and Ruthie's son was named Robin. Diana's husband who was an Israeli fellow, developed testicular cancer and died a short time after their son was born. When Ruthie's son, Robin, was around nine, Nat told her that business was not doing so well, and he was moving his business to Birmingham. He had a business partner there, and began staying there all week and would only come home on weekends.

Our cousins kept telling Ruthie to go to Birmingham and check things out; they suspected he was having an affair. Ruthie did not want to check it out at first, but later decided to do so. One day Nat's manager called her. She asked him if the housekeeper was in Birmingham with him. That's how she found out that he was living a double life. Their last housekeeper apparently was attracted to him, or so he thought. She was in love with his money, which he did not suspect. He set her up in Birmingham, and Ruthie found out that they had a child together.

When Nat's manager called her, she asked, "Is there anything I need to know?" He then told her that Nat brought the housekeeper back from France, he bought her a house, and they had a baby together. Her daughters would go visit and did not tell her what her husband was doing behind her back.

Ruthie and Nat finally divorced. A builder, who needed their home location as an entrance to a new subdivision he was building, purchased the Scandinavian house and swimming pool. The house was demolished to create the entrance road to the new subdivision, which he named after them, Grant Chester. Their last name is Grant.

Ruthie wrote a book called, *From Bitter Came Sweet*, relating her life experiences, and how she found God and spirituality and a devotion to Sai Baba, the Indian guru. Her book was published in 2004. (ISBN 81-87694-09-2) It is a very good book about her spiritual life.

Chapter Nine

Back to Meeting Luc Chaltin the Homeopath

When I met Luc Chaltin in October 1989, he prescribed homeopathic remedies for my health problems and also introduced me to eating healthy. He only ate organically grown food, and I trusted his advice. I changed my eating to a totally organic food diet. Slowly, my symptoms went away. My ulcer healed, and the pain in my left foot disappeared. I no longer had to use over-the-counter remedies, I also forgot that I ever had low back pain; it just went away. I became a believer in the healing power of homeopathy and eating organically grown food.

The timing of meeting Luc was perfect for both of us. Luc lived in a rented apartment in Lithonia; and his lease was about to expire in December 1989. I needed help with paying the mortgage and tuition to Emory University for my son. In December 1989, Luc moved in with me. We were a couple and he paid half the rent.

Luc than rented a storefront office space to use as a lab in Lithonia, and I quit my job at the personnel agency and focused my energies on making his lab a reality and a profitable business.

Luc was still travelling to Indiana, Ohio, and Kentucky and surrounding areas to see his patients every three months. I told him, that I would help him generate income with the lab, and he would no longer need to travel so far by car to earn a living. I did accompany him several times on his trips.

Part of Luc's healing regimen was emphasizing the importance of changing one's lifestyle and eating habits. It became my role to do this portion of educating his patients, I was more patient in explaining this new way of lifestyle to his patients than he was, and he appreciated my taking over this portion and being his partner.

What is Homeopathy?

Homeopathy is a complete system of healing discovered more than 200 years ago by the German doctor, Samuel Hahnemann. It has since been developed into a sophisticated science of diagnosing and prescribing, offering a wide variety of different homeopathic remedies to use in the healing process. The homeopathic remedies are all natural. They are made from minute amounts of substances from the vegetable, animal, and mineral kingdoms and they have no harmful side eff ects.

Homeopathy has healed millions of people since its inception in 1790. It is very successful throughout Europe and large parts of the world, and its use and acceptance is continually increasing. The British Royal family always travels with a homeopathic first aid kit and have always used homeopathy for their medicine.

Today, homeopathy is well-recognized and accepted because millions of Americans have discovered its benefits. Homeopathy has many benefits when compared to other healing systems. Homeopathy is effective. Scientificallyconducted double-blind tests have proven thousands of times that homeopathy helps all kinds of ailments, acute and chronic. It is safe and economical. It is far less expensive than drugs and it has an unlimited shelf life. It is not toxic like drugs and does not compromise one's liver and kidneys as toxic drugs do. Homeopathy is also approved by the FDA.

Creating a New Name and Logo for Our Homeopathic Remedies

Luc's idea for his business was to focus on selling his homeopathic remedies to health practitioners. I suggested that a better way to grow the business was to introduce it into health food stores. Luc agreed, and I proceeded to change the name, which Luc had originally called Purple Daisy, to Newton Homeopathics, and also changed the color and design of the label and logo.

We created a new brochure focusing on health food stores and I began to call on local Atlanta stores to introduce them to our product. I managed to open several accounts, and then proceeded to call on health food stores nationally and suggested to Luc that we attend industry conventions, which we did. This became the birth of Newton Labs, which I am proud to have co-created.

The business grew at a rate of around 25% to 35% the first year, and Luc no longer needed to travel far to see patients to supplement his income.

Wedding Date set for June 10, 1990

It was time to move again. I sold my condominium apartment, and we rented a ranch house in Snellville for six months.

Our wedding took place in a Middle Eastern restaurant across the street from Northlake Mall and lots of my friends attended. It was a lovely affair. My friend Tricia McCannon took the wedding pictures.

Luc had 10 children with his first wife, which he divorced sometime before he moved to the U.S. and to Atlanta. He than married his second wife, Helen, whom he met in Belgium, and she came to the U.S. with him. When I met Luc, he had just divorced his second wife and was looking for the third wife, I guess.

For our honeymoon, we flew to Belgium first. Luc wanted me to meet his children; he had ten, but was only on speaking terms with five of them. His children liked me and thought I was a good influence on Luc. It was a lovely visit and after a few days in Belgium, we flew to Israel to visit with my mother and my friends. We toured Israel, and Luc and I enjoyed our honeymoon.

Looking for a House to Accommodate the Lab

Upon our return from the honeymoon, I began looking for a house for us. It had to have enough room to be a home as well as a lab. My real-estate background came in handy at this time.

I found the perfect house for us in Conyers, Georgia. It had been on the market for about a year and seemed to be just waiting for us. It was a ranch-style house with a full daylight basement, four bedrooms, large living room, a sunroom, dining room, kitchen, two bathrooms and a large deck overlooking 15 acres of land bordering the Yellow river.

We purchased this home located at 612 Upland Trail, Conyers, GA for $145.000. I paid the closing cost and down payment of $15,900, since Luc did not have money, nor did he have the credit history needed to qualify for a mortgage. The closing was on November 15, 1990.

We moved into the house in November. Luc was very handy and strong for his age, which was 12 years older than me. Luc and my son finished the basement so that it would meet the criteria needed for a lab.

In the meantime, I was busy making sales calls to health food stores to introduce them to our homeopathic line, and have them carry our products. We had two employees in addition to Luc and me. Since we lived in a residential neighborhood, we needed to change the zoning in order to operate the business legally. I took the necessary steps to change the zoning, which was approved. We were legal!

Luc also prepared the soil to plant an organic garden. He grew lots of vegetables, and it was great to walk into the garden and pick cucumbers, tomatoes, corn, lettuce, peas, squash, watermelons, strawberries and more.

The next year our business grew at a rate of 35%. We paid ourselves very small salaries and put the profits back into the business and into savings for the future growth and expansion of the business. By 1993, with the growth of the business, we needed to expand the basement space, which we did, and we also hired my son Scottie, also known as Robert Scott Bell, as a full time employee.

Prior to hiring Robert Scott, he was studying homeopathy with Luc, and took to it like a fish to water. He became Luc's clone in a sense. It seemed that Robert Scott was born to be a homeopath. He absorbed the principals and they passionately worked well together. Robert Scott helped in taking Newton Labs to the next level by creating educational materials and teaching seminars for health food store owners and employees. His teaching and marketing skills were the catalyst for making Newton Labs a national business.

Luc's knowledge was that of a genius, but he had poor customer relation skills and was emotionally volatile. Robert Scott, on the other hand was very balanced, easy going, and a natural peacemaker. He buffered Luc's intense, angry, and impatient personality and helped heal injured relations Luc caused with patients and clients.

I learned to cook and eat only organically grown food, and since our lab was in the basement, the smell of good food would permeate the entire house. I would share my cooking with the stuff at lunch time, and they enjoyed it, especially my soups.

My Tumor and the Body's Ability to Cure Naturally

My health had much improved, however I had a marble-sized tumor on my back. Whenever my daughter hugged me, she felt that tumor. It did not bother me, nor was it painful, but she was concerned about it and said that I should go to a doctor to have it checked. I told her that Luc said not to worry, so I did not worry.

After about a year, the tumor began to grow, became red around the edges, and became painful. It grew in size and looked like a nasty carbuncle. It seemed that my body became strong, due to the healthy lifestyle and the use of homeopathy, and the body began to reject the tumor naturally. The tumor eventually opened up and by squeezing it, it drained extensively for quite some time. My son said that you could drive a Buick through it. It took several months until my body expelled all the toxins that had congregated in that one spot.

I have no doubt that had I not changed my lifestyle to organic food, and taking homeopathic remedies to help my body heal, I would have become a candidate for cancer. In giving the body what it needed, it became strong and able to throw out the accumulated toxins from a wrong lifestyle in a natural way without any surgery or drugs.

Nature is wonderful, if you stick to the laws of nature, your body can heal. It does take time, though. From what

I experienced through homeopathy and eating organic food, I became a true believer. Now, at age 79, I take no drugs whatsoever, not even aspirin. I rely on natural supplements, and I am feeling great.

Newton Lab is Growing

By 1995, the basement space became too small for the business. Luc and I discussed the need for a new lab to be built to our specifications. I began to look for the right piece of land because it had to be in an environmentally clean location. I located a great property for us, less than two acres in a clean industrial park in Conyers.

We purchased that property and paid cash for it with savings from the business. We closed on this purchase in January 1995 at 2360 Rockaway Industrial Boulevard, Conyers, Georgia 30012. Newton Labs is still there today.

Luc drew up the plans for the lab, and we hired a builder and got a construction loan from Main Street Bank, which was later converted into a mortgage.

Living and working with Luc, I experienced highs and lows. As a husband, he was like Dr. Jekyll and Mr. Hyde; I never knew whom I was dealing with. I had to walk on eggshells, not knowing what would rub him the wrong way or what would trigger his anger. He would explode and be very abusive. When that happened, I would move out of our bedroom to the guest room for the night, and would not speak to him.

He seemed clueless as to his abusive behavior and would be angry with me for leaving the bedroom. In the morning, he would stand at the door of the guest bedroom when I was still in bed and would just stare at me. He could not understand why I would not have sex with him. We would eventually make up, but this pattern repeated itself.

In business, we got along well. We complemented one another, and made for a good partnership. He was often rude to patients and clients, and I would pacify them by excusing his rude behavior due to the fact that he was a genius and a great healer and he did not mean to hurt their feelings.

We attended tradeshows nationwide, which specialized in natural modalities, such as the Natural Products Expo. I would make all the arrangements and schedule both Luc and Robert Scott to give lectures on homeopathy and natural healing. We were a successful team.

CAMA – Complimentary Alternative Medical Association and M. R.

> M. R. was president of CAMA. Luc and I were good friends with her and supported M and CAMA financially, and I donated my time as well. We believed in the mission of CAMA.
>
> CAMA's Mission:
>
> "Committed to educating the consumer; practitioner, and policy-maker about natural healing and health.
>
> Advancing the practice of complementary/ alternative medicine,
>
> Motivating consumers to take charge of their health, and
>
> Advocating freedom in health care choices."

M. worked at the VA hospital as an RN. The CAMA meetings were held once a month at the VA auditorium.

M. also had a room at the Georgia Capital donated to alternative medicine; the room was manned by alternative practitioners. The Georgia Medical Association also had a room at the capital, and was very well financed by the drug companies. They were able to wine and dine the legislators so that their agenda would be the one supported by legislating laws pertaining to medicine. However, alternative medicine had a difficult time competing with this financially-endowed giant supported by the drug companies. Since Newton Labs was a homeopathic lab and a holistic modality to medicine, we supported M. in her quest to educate the legislators. This is how we became involved with M. and supported her and her activities. She would educate the legislators on the benefits of natural healing and acupuncture and once a year she would have a holistic health fair at the Georgia Capital. Luc asked me to assist M. which I did. We also brought M. with us to tradeshows we attended. She occasionally drove with us if they were held in Orlando, or fly with us when it was in Las Vegas or other states. She would share a room with me at the hotel to help minimize her expenses. She was a friend.

I helped M. produce an annual CAMAFEST and produced an Annual Anniversary Gala. I will quote here some of the thank-you letters M. sent me to illustrate our friendship.

Letter dated November 6, 1999

Miki Bell
Newton Labs
2360 Rockaway Ind. Blvd.
Conyers, GA 30012

Dear Miki,

Nothing compares to true friends. No words are adequate to express my gratitude to you for your generosity, and for your support. I send you my sincere "Thank You" for the many hours you spent coordinating "CAMA's Third Anniversary GALA Celebration."

Everything was done with excellence, bringing elegance and charm to the entire occasion.

The Gala could not have been the huge success that it was without you. Everyone was complimentary, and I was delighted. Kudos to you!

On behalf of the Board of Directors, members and friends of CAMA, thank you for your support, your time, and your generous efforts toward making our Gala a night to remember. Most importantly, I truly value your friendship, Miki. Your generosity will be remembered for all time.

With kind regards,
M. R.

A note sent to me by M. dated June 2000, reads:

Miki,

Wanted to personally thank you for your faithfulness and years of hard work with CAMA.

I know I can always count on you to come through and go the extra mile.

You are truly a blessing not only for CAMA, but a privilege to know you on a personal basis.

Love, M.

Another letter sent to me dated Sept. 2001:

> *Dear Miki,*
>
> *On behalf of CAMA, I want to formally thank you for all your hard work in making CAMA Fest 2001 a success. And on behalf of Marge, I want to thank you for being there. You are such a great friend and it gives me a certain peace-of-mind among the chaos knowing I can always count on you. I know I can call on you and get a second opinion, a confirmation of an idea or a different perspective to think about.*
>
> *So thank you again for being there, for being you and for never wavering in your support of CAMA, of me and of the cause of natural medicine and freedom of choice.*
>
> *Love,*
>
> *M. R., RN, MSHP*
> *President/CEO, CAMA*

In 2001 I was asked to serve on the Board of CAMA, and the Board of directors welcomed me as a new member.

Chronology of Events with Luc and Newton Labs

By 1996, Robert Scott had developed teaching seminars for health food storeowners. This helped get the word out about our products and built a very loyal customer base nationwide.

During this time, the personal relationship between Luc and me was very rocky. Luc grew up in Belgium and was a child during World War II. He was born out of wedlock to his parents who later got married. However, the stigma of having been born a "bastard" to his parents, affected the way they treated him.

He complained that his mother never held him on her lap nor showed any love to him. He was starving for love as an adult, without really knowing it. He was also a sickly child, and his parents thought he was just lazy; hence, he grew up a wounded soul, in spite of the fact that he was very intelligent.

I was Luc's third wife (or third victim of his rage). He was taking his rage from childhood and subconsciously using it against his wives. However, he was an outstanding homeopath and a very gifted healer.

In 1965, he was gravely ill with tuberculosis. The doctors were not able to help him, so he consulted with a homeopathic doctor who told him, "You cannot cure tuberculosis with homeopathy." Unwilling to accept this, he went on a self-healing search and found the only book ever written in French on how to cure tuberculosis with homeopathy. He followed the book's instructions to a T. It emphasized liver detox, and within six months he had cured himself. This experience turned him into a believer in homeopathy. He made this his mission, and he became a gifted homeopath.

In 1996 Luc and I divorced, however, I continued in my position as Vice President of Newton Labs until the latter part of 2002, when I retired.

In 1999, Luc decided to give Robert Scott 10% stock in the company, to thank him for his dedication and commitment to the business, and for helping the business grow. It was his intentions to have Robert Scott inherit the business once Luc retired, as he was a natural to fill that position for Newton Labs.

By 2000, Robert and Luc started a radio show, Jump Start Your Health; their combination of intelligent and congenial chemistry was a hit. The show became syndicated in 75 different markets, helping to increase Newton's profile and customer base nationwide.

By 2002, Luc's relationship with Robert Scott became rocky. Luc felt that business was at a standstill and not increasing in sales, and he blamed this on Robert Scott. I tried to explain to Luc that after the 9/11 tragedy, all businesses were suffering, and it affected every industry. But Luc turned a deaf ear to what I was saying.

Unbeknown to me at the time, M. R. had shown interest in inheriting Newton Labs, and she was becoming Luc's confidante behind my back. Earlier in 2002, we attended a trade-show in Las Vegas. M. flew with us, and she shared a room with me in a villa we rented for all of us. Luc became very ill with excruciating abdominal pain. M., Luc, and I flew back to Atlanta together. Luc had to be wheeled in a wheelchair. We got him home, but he refused to see a doctor. He thought it was an intestinal issue and he was going to cure it himself.

We all took turns in taking care of him, including M. Luc's grandson, Markus, stayed overnight with Luc, and it was lucky he did, because when Luc got up at night to go to the bathroom, he fell and passed out. Markus called an ambulance and he was rushed to Rockdale General Hospital, where they discovered he had an inflamed prostate, and his bladder was about to burst.

After Our Divorce

In 1996, our divorce became final and I moved out of our home. It became impossible for us to live under the same roof, and I purchased a house to be built in Covington. During the time my dream house was being built, I lived with Robert Scott and my daughter-in-law, Nancy. It took about three months to complete and I moved into the new home built for me.

I loved that house. It was a lovely ranch-style with three bedrooms, two bathrooms, a sunny kitchen with an eat-in-area and a bunk seat by the bay window overlooking a lovely and rustic back yard, which I had fenced with cedar wood. I had several dogwood trees and planted blueberry bushes and some tomato plants as well. I continued working at Newton Labs and cherished my new serene environment.

On March 1, 1998, I was inspired to write the first and only poem I have ever written:

Life is a celebration if you choose it to be.

Life is the pits, if you choose it to be.

I am thankful for the pains of the past.

Forcing me to grow, and learn, that life can be what I want it to be.

I am in charge.

Life is a celebration.

I am celebrating the freedom I learned, through spiritual wisdom.

Growing every day, I welcome every change,

For complacency has no place in my space.

Love, trust, and freedom to truly be me are what I choose to be.

I am liberated from EGO, what a relief to be me…

Little did I know in 1998, how many more battles and betrayals still lay ahead for me to experience.

Back to Luc's Illness and M.'s Betrayal 2001-2002

After the episode of Luc's illness, he was never the same. His memory faded, and he did not remember who was taking care of him. M. took advantage and encouraged him to fire Robert Scott, and I was asked to retire. M. took over the lab, and I became a persona-non-grata.

I received a letter from M.'s attorney that I was no longer welcome in the lab, and should I show up, she would call the sheriff to escort me off the premises. Luc sued Robert Scott and me for fraud. This continued for a couple of years. The cost to us in attorney's fees to defend ourselves was very high. This whole incident was a shock, to say the least. What did we do to deserve this? Absolutely nothing. M. had an agenda to inherit Newton Labs and she succeeded.

Once we were out of the picture at Newton Labs, M. was paying herself and Luc a very high salary, plus a car, and she hired her boyfriend, who had no knowledge of homeopathy, nor any interest in it, except to cash his paycheck. Luc gave M. Power of Attorney, and she was in charge with Luc's blessings.

Although we were divorced, we worked well together in business, and I would invite Luc every year on his birthday to my home to celebrate his birthday. I would bake an organic cake and have candles for him to blow out. M. was always present as well as my children.

In May 2003, for Luc's 80th birthday, which was before all hell broke loose, I threw a surprise party for him. It was evident then that Luc could not remember much of what happened to him the past year. He was unaware of all the love and support around him from all of us. He just trusted M. at this point.

All of M.'s beautiful letters to me meant nothing. She had inherited Newton Labs. However, I had 35% stock and Robert Scott had 10% stock, and Luc had 55% stock.

Luc gave M. his stock in exchange for receiving a salary of $100,000 a year. I sued him, since in our divorce agreement, I was to have "first right of refusal" if he chose to sell his stock and vice-versa. I was willing to buy his stock.

The judge agreed that Luc had to take back his stock from M., but did not allow me to exercise my right of first refusal to buy his stock. This was what I wanted and should have been given that option. There is no justice in the legal system in my opinion. It didn't really change anything whether he or she held the stock, since M. was running the business anyway.

We devoted years to the business, put our hearts, energy, and labor into making it a successful and viable business. We paid ourselves meager salaries and invested most of the profits back into the business, and now when we should be reaping the benefits of our labor, M. was taking it all to herself without having put a dime into it. And she had the nerve to sue us!

She has to live with her conscious if she has one. I would not want to walk in her shoes. What goes around comes around, and one day she will get hers.

Around 2007, M. moved Luc into her home in her basement apartment, and later moved him to a bungalow on her property. She isolated him from all the people that admired, appreciated, and cared for him so that she could keep complete control over him.

Luc Chaltin Dies

In December of 2008, Luc tripped on a tree root while taking a walk on her property, according to M. He was taken to a hospital by ambulance and was operated on for a broken hip. The operation was a success, but the next day he died of an aneurism.

M. informed me of his death with a phone call.

While we were married, and even after our divorce, I included Luc in the social life we created with many friends and admirers. When M. took over, she isolated him so that she could keep her grip and control over him.

It was so sad that at the funeral home. As he lay there, there were just a handfull of people. His two daughters who came in from Belgium, M., a couple of employees and one customer plus me and two friends who were friends with Luc and myself.

What a sad ending to someone who was so highly regarded and admired as a gifted healer, who healed so many people over the years. In contrast, at the memorial of my first husband George Bell, who died one month after Luc, there were at least 200 people honoring him with their presence. George died of a kidney failure. He had been on dialysis for some time, and it was too much for him to endure.

In May 2009, we finally arrived at an agreement with M. to sell her our stock. She is now the sole and complete owner of Newton Labs. With her at the helm, the history, what made Newton Labs what it is, has been erased by her.

Chapter Ten

Looking to Meet Someone

November 2003

I logged into Match.com hoping to meet someone—I was ready to start dating. I got a reply from John James, a widowed gentelman. We talked on the phone first, and I found out that he lived in Covington, about a 5-minute drive from my house. We decided to meet. It was a very nice match, and we liked each other. He was a lovely person, and we began to date. He had been married to his high school sweetheart since he was 18; she had died of cancer after a long illness.

He had never been to the theater, or to concerts. I introduced him to the arts and he loved it. We enjoyed each other's company. After dating for three months, he suddenly got sick. It started with an infection in his toe, which did not heal. He was hospitalized, and within a few days he died.I was brokenhearted. He was such a nice person, and we had such a short time together. At his funeral, I met his daughter and grandchildren. I cried so much; I really missed him.

2004 - I Am Introduced to Executive Suite Singles

My girlfriend, Ann Olk, whom I met when I had my singles organization, called me and said she had attended a senior singles organization called, Executive Suite Singles or ESS for short. She thought I should check it out, so I did. I went and liked the people, so I joined and am still a member of this organization today.

I am so grateful for having been introduced to ESS when I was. I met wonderful ladies who became my good friends, especially Helen and Ann. I also made some very nice male friends especially John and Gerry. They became like my extended family. We would travel together and meet at times to play games or go dancing. The ESS environment is very friendly and supportive and not at all like a singles "meat market."

ESS meets once a week on a Wednesday from 5:30 p.m to 7:00 p.m for cocktails, camaraderie, and sometimes dinner as a group. Currently they meet at the 57 Squadron on Clairmont Road in Atlanta.

For a senior single person who may be widowed or divorced and would like to create a social life, I highly recommend checking us out. People are very friendly, and one can choose the activity of interest to them. There is a golf group, a book club group, a bridge group, a hiking group, a dancing group and many other activities to choose from. Check them out on their web site which is: *www.executivesuitesingles.org*

During the first year of my membership they had scheduled a cruise to Europe. I decided to join them, and met some wonderful people, and made new friends. I am thankful for this organization and the friends I made there. However, I have not yet met the man I would like to date.

My friends are precious to me, and I enjoy a very nice social life with activities like dancing, tennis, playing RummiKube (a tile game), travelling, water aerobics, etc.

These social activities took me into Chamblee and Buckhead, which was a long way from Covington, and I began to realize that it was time to move nearer to Atlanta. When I was working at Newton Labs, the trip to work was short, and I did not often go to Atlanta. I believed I would live the rest of my life in the house I had built in Covington.

It was clear to me that it was time to be closer to my social activities and friends, so in 1995 I put my house on the market, and hired the realtor who listed my house for sale. I asked her to show me homes in the Norcross area. I liked Norcross; it has a beautiful historic center and was conveniently located to my social activities.

The realtor showed me a new subdivision of townhomes in Norcross. The subdivision was still being built, it was charming, European-looking with three-sided brick, and it had a lot of personality. I liked the floor plan as well as the location. It was also planned to be a gated community which was important to me. I selected an end unit I liked. My daughter helped me pick this unit, and from my bedroom window on the second floor I have a view of the lake.

It has three bedrooms, 2½ baths, a galley kitchen, living room, dining room and a two-car garage, with a patio in the back. It has lots of closet space and a large pantry in the kitchen; it is just perfect for me. It is a quiet neighborhood and convenient to everything I need. My two cats, Tulip and Rosie, love it also.

I signed a contract on an end unit, and at the same time we found a buyer for my house. I moved to my new townhouse in November 2005. I am still living there and love it.

Chapter Eleven

Dating and Dancing

The friends I made through ESS would often go dancing at a club called The Getaway. We would go there after our Wednesday meeting. It is a very friendly place where everybody knows everyone, and even the staff knows everyone by name. It is safe, friendly, and enjoyable. It is located in the lower level of an office building in Chamblee and has been in this location for the past 30 years. It has a dance floor, a bar, and a TV to view the games and tables and chairs surrounding the dance floor.

Rick, the DJ, played mostly '50s dance music. I often danced with Bill who was always there, sitting at the bar and watching the ball game on the TV. On occasion he would take a break from the game and invite me to dance, and other ladies as well.

Bill was in the process of getting a divorce from his third wife, whom he had also met at the Getaway. When his divorce became final, he asked me out. I liked him; he was fun to dance with and to be with. We enjoyed dancing, good food, going to the movies or watching TV, and we shared the same political views and a mutual attraction for each other. Bill was an avid golfer, which I tried. I bought all the necessary gear, and took golf lessons, but I did not enjoy it that much. I might still take it up again one of these days.

Bill and I dated for close to two years. We were of the same age and are both in good shape for our age. He was about to retire, and he decided to move to the Villages in Florida. In September 2010, I threw a going-away party for him at the Getaway.

I do miss him and his company. We met a couple of times after he moved. He came back to Atlanta once around Christmas 2010, and I went to the Villages once to visit. The Villages is like a Disney World for seniors. It is surrounded by beautiful landscaping, lakes, golf courses, restaurants, and beautiful homes. Everyone drives around in their golf cart and the center of town in the evening has a band playing and people dance in the streets. It's like a carnival almost daily. Everyone is a senior and retired, and they all play golf daily, and then have cocktails starting at 4:00 p.m. I am not a drinker, and golf did not catch my interest, so I would not care to live there. It is perfect, however, for Bill and other seniors who are golf addicts. I am sure that by now Bill has found another lady. We email one another sometimes, just to stay in touch. He will always be a friend, and he is a very sweet and kind person.

I have not yet found a replacement for Bill, but I am not really looking, either. I am grateful and satisfied with the friends I have from ESS and the friends I made dancing West Coast Swing at the ASDC Club.

ASDC - Atlanta Swing Dancers Club

Since I love to dance, and I used to dance mostly ballroom dances like the cha-cha, swing, rumba, tango and waltz. I was not familiar with West Coast Swing. About three years ago, I was introduced to it, and fell in love with West Coast Swing. It is beautiful and very versatile and quiet different from East Coast Swing. I began taking group lessons, but found it hard to adapt to the different steps, so I took some private lessons with Pat Korn. The private lessons helped me get over the initial learning challenge and I found the WCS to be most enjoyable.

Every Sunday evening we danced WCS at Nemo's on Peachtree Parkway in Norcross. Check out our web site: *www.atlantaswingdancers.com*

A dance community exists in just about every city. Check out your local dance community, you are bound to meet very friendly and nice people who will make you feel welcome.

The Atlanta dance community is very active with very nice people, both single and married. Some met while dancing, got married and continue to dance; some met dancing and never came back. It's different for different people.

Dancing and Health Philosophy

I would highly recommend dancing as a healthy activity. Whether you are male or female, widowed or divorced, if you are sitting at home feeling sorry for yourself, get up and join your local dance community. There are dance lessons available, and many places to dance and meet friendly and caring people. Check out the Internet—and go dance. It will bring a smile to your face, and your body will thank you for it. Dancing is living in the moment and enjoying the moment.

The secret to living a happy life is living in the moment and not worrying about "what if." Things have a way of working themselves out when we get ourselves out of the way and enjoy the present. Trust and believe that whatever happens is for a reason. We may not see it when we're in the midst of it, but time always proves that there was a lesson to be learned, and if we learn that lesson and make a change, a better outcome awaits us.

Another secret to a happy life is not blaming others, but taking responsibility for our part in whatever happened. The choices we make create the outcome we get. Take responsibility and be in charge of your life.

I am told I look great for my chronological age of 79, and I am told I look at least 10 years younger than my age. I feel great and am active with no ailments, thank God. I play tennis and do yoga and water aerobics, in addition to my dancing, of course.

I have a very close and loving relationship with my daughter now, for which I am so grateful. She looks after me, and I look after her. She lives just a 30-minute drive from me, and we see each other at least once or twice a week. I am always available if they need me; they are my priority. I am close to my two grandsons Jeremy and Ben. I am not ecstatic about her involvment with Jehovah's Witnesses, but it makes her happy, so I am okay with that.

My son, Robert Scott Bell, and his family live in Florida. We talk once a week, and I visit them twice a year. They are very happy there and I am happy for them. I just wish they lived closer so that I could see my grandkids Elijah and Ariana more often than twice a year. But it is what it is, and I make the best of what is.

My cousin, Berni Lind, celebrated his 70th birthday in December 2011. The celebration was an elaborate affair over two days in West Palm Beach, Florida. My sister, Ruthie, came from London to attend the celebration, and I drove with her to West Palm Beach from Atlanta. It was such a lovely affair, and we got to meet Berni's side of the family, his children and grandchildren. Scottie and his family came for the goodbye breakfast Berni hosted for all his guests. We later drove to Fort Lauderdale to visit with Scottie, and my sister and I spent two days with them before returning to Atlanta. We drove back all the way to Atlanta, a 12-hour drive. My sister was amazed that at my age I could drive 12 hours. She said I deserve a medal. Well, my medal is my good health at my age.

I remember that before I met Luc, I was suffering from lower back pain in addition to my other ailments, and the longest I could sit without experiencing pain was half an hour, I would than have to get up, stretch, and walk around to reduce the pain which was quite severe. Now I can drive 12 hours straight with no pain anywhere whatsoever. I think this is a testament to a good and healthy living.

I am at a calm period of my life now for which I am grateful. I don't take on more than I can handle. I am relaxed, and I enjoy the fact that I no longer have to fight the battle of survival which accompanied me most of my life.

I appreciate the fact that I no longer suffer from stress in my body, which was the case when I was married to Luc. I often suffered from a stiff neck and upper back pain, although he helped relieve my ailments, he caused my body stress due to his energy and anger. I would often go to chiropractors and massage therapy, but it didn't help much. I now know that the cure was to get out of the marriage which I did.

In 2012, a presidential election year, I became involved with the Georgia Conservative Republican party, and I was elected delegate to the county and the state conventions. Being involved in the political system left me with a sour taste in my mouth. It seems that so much of it is about power and control, rather than being committed to doing the right thing for our country. I was a Ron Paul supporter, and I found his views and actions a breath of fresh air. It was unfortunate that he did not win.

I have also served on the board of the Atlanta West Coast Swing club this year as second vice president. My service on the board will end at the end of this year. I like the club and its members, and it is time for other people to come forward and serve.

I am giving myself permission to take it easy and just serve Miki at this point in my life. I feel amazed and exhausted from writing about my life and how many struggles I endured and never gave up. I hope to leave a legacy to my grandchildren that hard work and commitment to be the best that you can be, no matter what, is an important aspect of one's character. Success is not measured in how much money you make, but how much you like yourself as a human being. You can not control how others view you or like you, but you can control how you like and feel about yourself.

My life's experiences and the many betrayals and challenges I endured made me the strong person that I am, and inwardly I am sensitive and caring. Whenever I hear a marching band, or view a happy or sad occasion that people are experiencing; my eyes automatically fill with tears. At that point I feel like an abandoned little girl of times passed. Maybe that is why it takes me a while to open up to people before I know them. I am usually more on the quiet side and do not share much of myself unless asked.

On July 14, 2013, my sister Ruthie will celebrate her 85th birthday. I plan on flying to London for the celebration and our sister, Nava, from Israel is also planning on attending. A big celebration is planned for about 60 people. Ruthie is also thankful for her good health as a very active 84 year old lady; we are both gifted with a youthful disposition.

Chapter Twelve

The Secret to Good Health and My Life's Philosophy

At age 78, I take no drugs, not even aspirin; I only take natural supplements which help keep me in good shape, young, and supple. I follow my son's recommendations and take the following supplements daily:

OMEGA 3, by Nordic Naturals:

www.nordicnaturals.com

ALTA SILICA, by Alta Health Products:

www.altahealthproducts.com

SELENIUM, by BioSan Laboratories:

www.innateresponse.com

MAGNESIUM, by BioSan Laboratories
I also take Dr. Ohhira's Probiotics 12 Plus, which is excellent for the digestive system.
If you would like to listen to my son's talk show which airs 6 times a week for two hours, you can log into: *www.robertscottbell.com*

The quality of the supplements is of utmost importance. If they are manufactured by a company that uses synthetic materials, the outcome will not be the same as when they are manufactured by a credible company that uses non-synthetic materials. The name may be the same, but it will not give the body the results desired. The process of manufacturing is also important in order to derive full benefits.

I trust the source I use and purchase my supplements from Choose to be Healthy at *www.choosetobehealthy.com* or 1-866-424-1077. F.Y.I.

Last summer, I suffered from rheumatic pain in my left hand. It was so painful that I had to bandage my hand. My son suggested I take my supplements, which I had not taken for some time. Within one week of getting back to taking my supplements, the pain was gone, and I now take my supplements regularly in order to avoid a repeat of the rheumatic pain.

I am a true believer in the natural and organic lifestyle. Several years ago, I had a McDonald hamburger. It tasted good while I ate it, but half an hour later my stomach was so upset, and my body rejected it by vomiting. I learned my lesson.

When our bodies are clean, and without all the artificial additives in food and chemicals in farming, they become sensitive to the wrong foods and automatically reject it. That is also the reason my body was able to reject the tumor I had on my back, which would have surely turned into cancer had I not changed my lifestyle and cleansed my body by eating only organic foods and not taking any chemical drugs that would have compromise my kidneys and liver.

Our medical society has become so specialized, ignoring the fact that everything is interconnected. Specialists are trained in their area of specialty. They do not look at the whole body to find the source of the problem and only treat the symptoms. Each one of us is unique, and what is right for one, may not be right for another. However, the medical profession lumps us all into categories, and then decides, based on averages, which drug will "improve" a condition, that may not fit the individual. Each one of us is not an average, we are each unique and should be treated as such.

I am sharing my experience in the hope that it will result in a healthier lifestyle and minimize the amount of drugs Americans are taking. As my son says, "The power to heal is yours."

It is statistically known that the average senior takes as many as seven different drugs a day for different ailments. I am sure that with improving the quality of one's food and working with more holistic practitioners, one's health can be greatly improved, and the amount of drugs taken can be gradually reduced. What a novel idea.

People complain that organic food is too expensive. I say that in the long run, it is cheaper, because as your health improves, you use fewer drugs, and you will not have to visit the doctor as frequently, and your body will thank you.

Your taste buds will also improve, and you will learn to differentiate between what is good for you, and what is not. How about that for a good outcome.

Our bodies are desensitized due to the chemicals used in farming and the hormones and antibiotics given to chicken and cattle. It is no wonder that today's children reach puberty so much earlier than we did as children. This is due to the hormones fed to chickens and cattle to expedite their growth and increase their weight. All this is in order to increase the profits with no regard to the long-term effects this has on our younger generation and society. It is pure greed with no regard to the damage it creates. The media is benefitting from the drug commercials, so they will not give you the truth about the benefits of holistic modalities.

Have you wondered why so many young children today are afflicted with cancer? This was not the case when we were growing up. In fact, cancer was quite rare in the '40s. The food was much healthier and cleaner. It was organic. This was before the introduction of chemicals and artificial colorings into our foods.

Make the best of your life in the now. Take responsibility for your choices and actions. If you don't like the results, you only have yourself to blame. Take charge, and live responsibly. Our society will be better for it, and so will your life. It's the only one you have for now, so enjoy, have fun and go dancing, or do whatever it is that makes you happy. If you are not happy, nobody around you is happy.

Spread your joy around. Usually, a happy body is a healthy body. This may sound too simplistic, however simple is always better than complicated. There is much truth in simplicity; nothing is covered up.

I hope I leave this world better than I found it so that my grandchildren's life is a better one than the one I had. However, there is much learned from hardship in life. We appreciate the good that comes our way much more than if we grew up being spoon-fed and overprotected. I am thankful for the hardships I endured; they made me the person I am today, and I like the person I am.

Be the best that you can be. The happiest people don't necessarily have the best of everything; they just make the most of everything they have.

I believe that our background and circumstances may have influenced who we are, but we are responsible for whom we become.

With much love,
Miki Z. Bell

Miki would love to hear from you, e-mail
her at: bell321@bellsouth.net

Made in the USA
Columbia, SC
26 January 2020

87161826R00087